D1733824

CHILDREN
OF
POVERTY

Studies on the Effects of Single Parenthood, the Feminization of Poverty, and Homelessness

edited by

STUART BRUCHEY
University of Maine

A GARLAND SERIES

ORGANIZATIONAL AND COMMUNITY RESPONSES TO DOMESTIC ABUSE AND HOMELESSNESS

MARJORIE BARD

GARLAND PUBLISHING, Inc.
New York & London / 1994

Library of Congress Cataloging-in-Publication Data

Bard, Marjorie.
    Organizational and community responses to domestic abuse and
homelessness / Marjorie Bard.
        p.   cm. — (Children of poverty)
    Includes bibliographical references and index.
    ISBN 0-8153-1597-X
    1. Abused women—United States—Psychology.   2. Homeless
women—United States—Psychology.   3. Abused women—Services
for—United States.   4. Homeless women—Services for—United
States.   I. Title. II. Series.
HV6626.2.B26   1994
362.82'928'0973—dc20   93-47244
                                                                              CIP

Printed on acid-free, 250-year-life paper
Manufactured in the United States of America

For the most wonderful mother in the world: Eleanore Balser Friedgood. Her loving support and consistent affirmation of my ability to overcome all obstacles permitted this hidden homeless woman to leave the shadows and spread a bit of [en]light[enment].

Contents

Introduction   ix

Acknowledgments   xix

  I.   Conceptualizing Domestic Abuse, Victimization,
       and Homelessness: Typifications, Implications,
       and Ramifications   3

  II.   "I've Never Told My Story to Anyone Before":
       Idionarrating and Life Events in Introspect and
       Retrospect   27

  III.   Victims' Narratives: Expression of Personal,
       Social, and Political Concerns   41

  IV.   Tell a Story, Start an Organization   85

  V.   Personal Narratives as Intervention Strategy in
       Intraorganizational Crisis   97

  VI.   Storytelling as Interorganizational
       Communicating: Paradigms and Problems   115

  VII.   Narrating, Transorganizational Networking, and
       Societal Needs   133

Exhibits: 1.   81
             2.   82

Bibliography   153

Index   163

Contents

Introduction

The text of this study remains virtually the same as written in 1988. The root causes of and posited solutions to domestic abuse and homelessness have not changed; however, the phenomena are so prevalent and publicized in the 1990s that few today question the material I presented to (too often) unbelieving public and academic audiences in the 1980s. Additions, therefore, include updated studies, statistics, activities, and commentary which relate to the hypotheses I formulated before I was able to become the full-time Executive Director of nonprofit, 501(c)3, Women Organized Against Homelessness (WOAH), working daily with the abused; pre-homeless; homeless; volunteer community members; paid public and private sector staff who provide human services; and advocates who seek better resources, services, housing, economic opportunities, and legislation.

While it is doubtful that there will ever be a consensus as to the quantitative aspects, it is obvious that life in the 1990s reflects social, economic, political, and philosophical changes which include varied family dysfunctions; systems inadequacies and failures; grassroots and public sector organizational activities; and community responses that range from local initiatives to wider public-private service/housing/business partnerships.

The qualitative aspects of this in-depth, long-term study connote a unique ethnography which, through thousands of personal experience narratives, creates an oral history that is far more revealing than the material that will appear in history books. My (second career) academic grounding in folklore provides a respect for the stories people tell about their private lives which other disciplines often denigrate as "not accurate" and therefore not useful as scholarly database, analysis, or interpretation. The many questions raised concerning domestic abuse and homelessness are diverse and usually not directly correlated by academics and their studies. Folklore is an almost 200-year-old discipline which attempts to understand how and why people have always expressed themselves—and therefore necessarily crosses interdisciplinary boundaries; it provides (in my opinion) the most open-minded path for investigative and interpretive research, particularly in regard to human behavior. Solving the problem of the usual constraints of any one discipline's prior scholarship, principles, or methodologies, I developed a set of questions and hypotheses that represent research in women's studies, psychology, sociology, anthropology, organizational development and behavior, urban and rural planning, social welfare, victimology, and law. I needed to investigate and interpret 1)why women remain in cohabitant situations while incurring inhumane treatment, 2) why, with a plethora of nonprofit organizations, there are none that I know of (aside from WOAH) comprised of ex-homeless, pre-homeless, and homeless women (mainly mid-life and without in-tow children) which specifically address unique problems, 3) why past and current assistance programs and laws have not stemmed the rise in domestic abuse or homelessness, and 4) from whom will innovative thought come and from what sources will solutions be provided that eliminate domestic abuse and homelessness—as separate phenomenon and as they correlate.

There have always been *obvious* answers to the first question, even before scholars in the fields of sociology, women's studies, social welfare, psychology, and victimology began to publish on the subject. Common sense directs our attention to historical, cultural, religious, social, political, and economic reasons why women have been repressed—if not oppressed—and as a result have become entrapped by lack(s) of opportunity(ies). But those answers never quite satisfied me; there was and is something else going on which has eluded definition and elucidation. I heard long stories from psychologically and physically abused wives which were essentially excuses for staying with men who treated their friends, co-workers, neighbors, and pets with more "like" and "love" than their mates. I heard myself making similar excuses; I remained wife because 1) "I know I can change him; he just needs understanding and another chance"; 2) "I think he really does love me but doesn't know how to show it properly"; 3) "He's under so much stress at work"; and 4) "I have no money now; where else could I go?"

I grew up with gentle and supportive parents and considerate friends. I had an excellent education. I had no religious qualms about divorce. I had two successful careers. Why did I stay with a man who constantly told me—and encouraged his four young children (my stepchildren) to tell me—that I was worthless, horrible, and unwanted? They certainly used my "worth": my loving and constant care, creative abilities, money, and housewifely performances. I had no doubts that they were cruel and liars; my self-esteem was high. And for all of the "studies" which delineate the *abuser* (as well as the abused) as possessive of low-esteem, other women and I note that many abusive males are truly secure individuals who are not masking feelings of low self-esteem. Further, most did not come from abusive families. In other words, many women and men simply do not exhibit the characteristics which most researchers attribute to them. So, if the "reliable" studies are not accurate for much of the abused and abuser population, why else *do* women stay in terroristic relationships—beyond the obvious aforementioned reasons of religion, economics, and cultural tradition?

I kept hearing women say: "But I'll be alone if I don't have him"; or "Well, he's better than not having a husband at all"; or "At least we're all together; the children need a father"; or "I'm going to keep us a family no matter what." While the reality of economics did entrap me, I also wanted a "family" enough to let five people use and abuse me. Other women are still doing the same thing. We are not masochists; we do not enjoy being hurt. All men are not misogynists or misogamists. Why do they not just *leave* women they dislike so much that they feel compelled to beat or denigrate? Men must also *need* "family." Could the concept of "family" be so important that all else blanches in comparison?

That seemed to be a hypothesis worthy of testing. If we, as *homo sapiens*, do have a need for such a tie-bonding, is that basic need so strong that we allow and condone unbelievable suffering? Perhaps that need is an unconscious one. We may express the need without necessarily understanding or being consciously aware of it.

There are many ways of expressing needs, hopes, and fears. One very common one is through the process of narrating. The study of narrating, narrators, and narratives has been of prime importance to folklorists. The *personal* narrative has been of particular interest to Sandra K.D. Stahl (1977, 1983, 1989) and establishes that form as a traditional manner of expression appropriate for scholarly pursuit. The personal experience narrative has been taken one academic step further by Eleanor Wachs in her examination of the crime-victim narrative: "While [these stories] may have evolved from a traditionally urban topic of conversation—that of crime linked to city life these narratives highlight the wedding of an important contemporary issue to that of the personal experience narrative" (1981: 17). This is the link I intend to pursue: the impact of the personal experience narrative in the discovery and delineation of and ways of dealing with societal problems and issues attendant to victimization and homelessness.

The first step I take is to investigate the manner in which individuals express personal concern; I suggest that *before* an individual relates a noteworthy experience to another person, she has *told herself that story*—and more often than not, she has repeated that silent performance many times: she has engaged in the act of self-communicating, or *idionarrating*, a process that I found to be of folkloric significance and shall treat in Chapter Two. The second step is to explore the link between victims' narratives (to others) and issues of personal, social, and political concern (Chapter Three). The third step is to study the relationship between storytelling and certain actions which *follow* narratives about societal concerns—actions which lead to the formation of organizations (Chapter Four). Chapters Five and Six deal with the communicative relationships within and between organizations which comprise the support and service networks responsible for the assistance of victims. Chapter Seven proposes models for collaborative interaction and constructive action to assist the homeless as well as utilize skills of populations heretofore neglected.

This study is not only a written documentation of personal and organizational accomplishments and failures, but also represents self-disclosure for the first time for many victims. I believe that the reader will discover that this is not a study that *any* scholar could have researched and written. My personal belief is that only someone who has experienced abuse and homelessness—who can identify with the abuse and torment which so many victims have endured—can gain the trust of such individuals in crisis. The context of my research is such that it would not have been possible for the researcher to step temporarily from one persona (the non-victim academic) into another which is completely foreign to him or her. There is no way one can "pretend" living in an abusive relationship, with its psychological distress and physical deterioration. One cannot pretend constant fear, frustration, or pain. Real nightmares cannot be invented in the imagination. An academic could feign homelessness for a determined period, but could always "go home" when the going gets rough.

What an academic *can* do, and here has done, is to devote endless hours to discovering and interviewing the abused and homeless (who, incidentally, are not all highly visible), and disclose and draw upon prior and current personal experience. Interviewing these populations is not in any way similar to face-to-face interaction with a songwriter, or a lumberjack, or a craftsperson. People in crisis are afraid: they place little confidence in others and usually do not wish their personal demons examined. Often they are in imminent danger of further victimization if they tell the truth.

Methodology, therefore, becomes of prime importance, as does objective analysis. There cannot be a single methodology in obtaining qualitative and quantitative data. There must be flexibility, patience, respect, and empathy in fieldwork—combined with an academic background in recognizing presuppositions, assumptions, and cultural biases and developing working hypotheses that are tested without prejudice. There must be an ability to have one foot in an academic shoe while the other foot still feels the pinch of pain from personal experience. The researcher must be able to conduct open-ended interviews at the will of the informant, listening to hours of discourse about everything one does not want to hear while awaiting the elusive disclosure that may even be unintentional. That really is at the crux of the matter: eliciting personal experience narratives about a particular subject. It is an art form in and of itself. It may sound easy, and indeed in many cases eliciting stories is easy, but not from individuals who assume you only want to hurt them. Their stories may be all that they have left of "themselves."

I have spent eighteen years interviewing frightened women in isolated surroundings (in four states) so as to protect anonymity and often life itself. Technique involved the vacuum-cleaner method: get everything you can from field informants and sort it out later. That brings up the matter of how I documented all of this material. It meant learning to use shorthand with one hand inside of a large paper bag or purse; writing on paper plates, sandwich wrappers, placemats, toilet tissue, envelopes, stones, and one rather expensive white skirt; remembering to keep extra batteries for two tape recorders— which while always in sight did not stare at my field informant like a third party; and foregoing a fear of cameras with more than "one step."

Most of the time a researcher must be in the right place at the right time with the right intuition and the right personality (and approach) for the right occasion. The old saying, "It takes one know one" is apt, and it usually takes the ability, before receiving any salient data, to disclose information of a personal nature in order to encourage the subject to relate freely. It is a variation on a proven field-technique of folklorists: tell a story to get a story. But one must tell the *right* story to elicit the story one wants. And after years of trial and error in obtaining data from people who become temporary "soulmates" during intimate discourse, the researcher realizes she should be looking at the quantitative side of analysis. However, it is not statistical data that interest me; I have sought instead the qualitative material which provides insights into the how and why of victimization and its consequences.

Until I experienced abuse and homelessness, both as an escalating "surprise" and with no one with whom to share my anguish, I had no insights as to the psychological and physical trauma involved in crisis situations. I did not know how to deal with the problems that are described over and over again by victims. One literally is alone; when people ask you, "How are you doing?" they do not want to hear the truth about personal dilemmas. In addition, community services that are loudly and proudly proclaimed by politicians (and others) often simply do not exist or do not work properly: "the system stinks" is a polite way of expressing what victims explicate. The thousands of field informants who have supplied me with data know of what they speak; they would not be in the state—or transitional stage of life—that they are in if they did not have first-hand knowledge of the facts.

I knew—and know—it myself. I can recall every exquisite detail of victimization by an abusive husband, and the insensitive and often outright corruptive behavior of attorneys, agency members, and public officials in Baltimore, Maryland, who contributed to the creation of a homeless person: me. I suspect that I may be the only woman who has survived psychological and physical torture; overt neglect and malfeasance by attorneys; lies by state, county, and court officials; [illegal] denial of access to the judicial system and my own divorce trial; and enforced indigency and homelessness to keep her sanity and sense of humor (an absolute necessity) and (re)enter graduate school to focus on the process of dual victimization: abuse by individuals and "the system."

It is a fair question to ask if I can be objective. My response is that even library research cannot be completely objective. Researchers look for what they want to find, hope to find it, and are pleased when they do. Questionnaires are certainly biased by the scholar's input. Statistical research is based on who (or what) one counts. None of this means that the academician must have a closed mind, ignore or change facts, or distort research results. If one has had excellent academic training in principle, methodology, and ethics (and I did during my experience at UCLA), one develops an alter ego who has *not* been affected by personal tragedy; one can create an "other self" that is the objective researcher—as much as any human can remain apart from the topic of his study. In addition, my data are not based on my own experiences—although I have documented the process of victimization which affected me because that documentation is so complete that it bears proof of what others claim but lack in written proof. I listened carefully and recorded exactly that which field informants disclosed. I examined all of the legal/judicial paperwork offered to me. And then I analyzed. That is what other scholarly researchers do. I simply had an advantage: I knew how to establish rapport with and elicit life stories from a truly distrusting and marginally invisible population. I had a hypothesis and I tested it: there is a relationship between domestic abuse and the new and rising population of female-homeless, and the only reliable way to gather reliable data is to gain substantial qualitative information through personal experience narratives. The correlation between domestic abuse and homelessness should not be a surprise to anyone; it simply has not been studied in a similar long-term, detailed, and academic pursuit.

I had other hypotheses: 1) we tell stories to ourselves before we narrate to others, 2) we often tell stories which become antecedents to action—in this case for creating organizations and social activism, 3) the telling of personal experiences is a particularly effective intervention strategy in organizational crisis, 4) narrating is an important form of inter-organizational networking, and 5) storytelling plays a significant role in trans-organizational development. Again, I based my hypotheses on the personal experience narratives of women who *lived* these personae and roles.

While I could not expect women existing in tenuous circumstances—in cars, malls, alleys, and parks—to carry among their few possessions complete certification of *their* victimization, I discovered that more than 90% *did* have written documentation—usually tattered from constant review—which proved victimization by individual and system and "the truth" of their stories. I have no reason, then, to doubt the ludicrous behavior (by attorneys and officials) alleged when there is no immediate written certification; there are just too many undeniable paper trails.

Many of my field informants remain in contact with me after they regain mainstream life. Some tell me about problems that occurred after leaving the shelter for battered women where I was house support staff or after the courtroom door slammed shut in the court system where I was a victim advocate for the city attorney's office. Others, now homemakers and/or business-women, reveal how tenuous "mainstream" life really is. Some women have become personal friends who now assist the needy through our nonprofit organization, WOAH. I have continuing correspondence with women who hear or see me via the media (newspaper and magazine articles, radio talk shows, and television segments such as "60 Minutes") and conferences regarding victims' rights, domestic abuse, affordable housing, community planning, and veterans' affairs. As a member of several film/television industry organizations, I am also in close contact with highly recognizable actresses, producers, directors, writers, and production staff who have been or currently are "between spouses" as well as "between jobs"; no one would suspect them of having personal knowledge of homelessness.

I feel competent to state that there are as many if not more invisible—undetectable—homeless women in the United States who are doubled-up with relatives or friends or live secretly out of vehicles than there are highly visible "street people" and those who are agency-recognized and therefore identifiable and counted. A majority of them have been forced to leave their homes, either voluntarily or involuntarily, because of family violence or emotional abuse. They prefer to remain anonymous while continuing to seek appropriate housing and employment, and they object strenuously to the concept that they are not "empowered" because they do not identify themselves for purposes of gaining welfare monies and public sector (almost always high-rise, poor/crime-ridden neighborhood) housing; they insist they *are* the "empowered" ones: women who will win over system failures—which include such rules as being forced to sell one's car if it is worth over $1,200, having no more than $100 to one's name, and owning no personal property worth over $1,000 (which means that a professional musician must sell her instrument to qualify for General Relief [welfare] in Los Angeles). Daily, I am contacted by women who hear of WOAH'S activities either by word-of-mouth from other victims or friends or from agencies which cannot perform the services that we do, e.g., retrofitting cars for more comfortable sleeping and storage, finding safe streets for nighttime parking, discovering the best Happy Hour (free food) restaurants, dealing with impound yard problems, updating yearly car license fees, providing private introductions for home and job sharing, creating cottage industries, and arranging for national relocations. In addition, I encourage the exchange of expensive cars for the "homelike" and greater-distance job-search/new life mobility of conversion vans and motorhomes. I constantly create new networks for alternatives to what have been considered to be "normal/usual" home ownership and employment.

I present the best possible argument for academics to value interdisciplinary research (library and fieldwork) and pursue qualitative studies in and of their own communities. After all, scholars are part of our society and often become victims themselves: abused in family settings or by legal/judicial/medical systems—and even experience unemployment which could lead to homelessness. Scholars are articulate, versed in the powers of persuasion, and are potentially influential beyond the ivory tower. They should be among the pro-active in organizational and community responses to domestic abuse and homelessness.

Acknowledgments

I owe a debt of gratitude to so many women who trusted me by sharing lifestories which often put their lives in jeopardy. They, as I, are vividly aware of retaliation. And so I publicly thank those whose stories appear in print and those whose private experiences remain part of a continuing ethnography and oral history.

I also wish to acknowledge the professors who, through their scholarship concerning narrators, narrating, and narratives, evoked my intense study of those who step momentarily from the shadows to express in all manner of emotions and styles the stories which reveal society's problems and solutions. I will never forget how Michael Owen Jones, Donald Ward, Robert Georges, and David Boje have altered my academic, organizational, and community pursuits.

Organizational and Community Responses to Domestic Abuse and Homelessness

Conceptualizing Domestic Abuse, Victimization, and Homelessness

This announcement appeared in the 28 October 1764 issue of the *South Carolina Gazette:*

> Lydia, the wife of John Wilson, having eloped from her husband; he hereby forbids all persons to give her any credit in his name, being determined not to pay any debt of her contracting...He likewise forbids the harboring or entertaining his said wife, on pain of prosecution.

At first glance, John Wilson has simply stated he will not be responsible for any debts incurred by his wife--who has abandoned him. However, John's last sentence contains information which provides singular insights into the social, economic, and political life of women in America in 1764. Lydia Wilson, once removed from her home—for whatever reason— had no ability to act freely within her own community, or indeed, in any other community unless she was an exceptional and economically-independent woman. The announcement implies that John owns Lydia as a piece of property, and anyone who helps to hide her is guilty of concealing John's chattel and is punishable by law.

Surely Lydia was a victim not only of a marital incident, but of the legal and service-provider systems of 1764. Emilio Viano, victimology scholar and editor of *Victimology: An International Journal*, notes that the concept of victim is an ancient one which appears in all cultures (1976). The English language contains a well-developed vocabulary pertaining to the notion of victim, e.g., victimhood, victimize, victimizable, victimization, victimizer, and victimless. Did Lydia conceive of herself as a victim? We could only know if we had some expression of her feelings and attitudes, such as those characterized by Sarah Cantwell in a notice in a 1776 *South Carolina American General Gazette* (which was on display in the 1976 Bicentennial Exhibition on Women in America from 1750 to 1815, in Plymouth, Massachusetts):

> John Cantwell has the Impudence to advertise me in the papers, cautioning all Persons against crediting me; he never had any credit till he married me: As for His Bed and Board he mentioned, he had neither Bed nor Board when he married me. I never eloped, I went away before his face when he beat me.

Women who expressed themselves publicly in the 1700s were bravely opposing customary behavior: behavior sanctioned by society and law. While English Common Law regarding wife-abuse (the "Rule of Thumb," in which a husband could beat his wife with a stick no thicker than his thumb) was no longer approved, an eighteenth-century wife's privileges were strictly defined by traditional role, social obligation, and economic dependence. It was expected that a woman would put up with her husband's foibles—including abuse—and, if a wife had the nerve to leave home, she would forfeit the personal, social, and economic rights afforded without question to men.

It can be assumed that Sarah Cantwell was not alone in her quest for "justice" in the 1700s. There must have been numerous other women who were forced from their homes and faced with insurmountable problems related to companionship, housing, economics, and politics. In the case of Sarah, one is prompted to pose a number of provocative questions. Are we (the reader) the first to hear her story? Was her motivation for such a sharp retort the result of John's impudence, or because she was faced with a lack of credit, housing, food, and former friends? What would she reveal in person that we miss via the printed page? How did she look (bruised?), and what mannerisms (fiddling, doodling?) and gestures (pointing?) did she utilize while telling her story? We can only guess at the tone, pitch, and intonation of her voice as she revealed what life with and after John was like. Did she tell just one brief story—or did she feel so self-or-audience stimulated that she told several in a row as part of a repertoire of stories of unacceptable behavior? Were any incidents revealed which included supranormal experiences? How did she make others "believe" her story(ies)? And finally, one is compelled to ask what happened to Sarah once she was forced from her home. Since it can be assumed that no one in the eighteenth-century documented Sarah's plight, the answers to these questions remain unknown. However, that which the contemporary researcher can do is to look at comparable cases from the present, and pose these same questions and seek to answer them.

We can formulate a hypothesis concerning domestic life in 1764: domestic violence may have led to indigency and homelessness for many females. What questions can be raised concerning domestic violence in the 1990s? Five come to mind at once: 1) What is the nature of and language concerning domestic violence? 2) Does victimization affect self-image, personhood, and identification; if so, how? 3) Does domestic violence lead to indigency and homelessness in contemporary America? 4) What are the implications and ramifications of the previous questions? 5) From what sources and in what manner can we best glean insights and form working hypotheses?

The typification of the "battered wife" as *physically* violated perpetuates the assumption that "battered" means a *hands-on* display of power by one person over another. Since the 1970s and the revival of the women's movement (sporadic movements for women's rights narrowly improved female status in regard to marriage, education, politics, and occupations from the late 1870s), emphasis has increasingly been placed on psychological or emotional abuse sustained by women in family disruptions. The most important is the recognition of the "battered woman syndrome." While I have not found a relevant study on "brief reactive psychosis," this phenomenon relates to the psychology of trauma—in amore radical form than the well-known and widely accepted post-traumatic stress disorder ("Hearings" 1990). Ann Jones cites particular cases in *Women Who Kill* (1980). Mary McGuire's husband, while teaching submission, made Mary watch him dig her grave, kill the family cat, and decapitate a pet horse. And then when she fled, he forced her to return by holding a gun to her child's head. The implication that physical attack is an *integral factor* in "domestic violence" still exists, however, by the utilization of the words "battered" and "violence." Clearly battering and violence do not properly characterize all cases of cruel treatment and abuse within the family milieu which women (and children) may have to endure or which directly lead to the female being compelled to leave home (often with children). *The Handbook of Family Violence* (1988) elaborates on statistics regarding the evidence of mental health problems of abused women in addition to physical injuries. Two points made are that 37% of such women have a diagnosis of depression or other situational disorder and at least one in ten abused women suffers psychotic breakdowns. At the Hearings Before the United States Senate Judiciary Committee (1990), it was submitted that battered women may also suffer a range of psycho-social problems, not because of illness, but only because of being abused. It was also concluded that women experience more episodes of depression than men due to their experience of just being female in our contemporary culture!

The disclosure of circumstances such as Sarah Cantwell's suggest that wives suffering from abuse—physical, perhaps, but also in the psychological sense alone—be recognized as victims of domestic "violence." Constant denigration, humiliation, neglect, or social or economic isolation can be as debilitating to a human being as physical abuse, but are not "violence" in its proper sense. It is apparent that current concepts and terms used to describe abuse of women need to be re-evaluated and re-placed by new terms and concepts. I further suggest that the inadequacy of these current concepts is symptomatic of an improper conceptualization of the entire phenomenon of the abused wife. "Domestic abuse," for example, is more appro-priate than "domestic violence," as is "abused wives" as opposed to "battered wives." The ramifications of altering language also provide for greater in-sights into specific populations and problems. Since secrecy is often an inherent factor in abusive families, members are intimidated; no one must discover what happens in the home, especially police or physicians. "No one will believe you" is a popular threat, and women are unlikely to reveal that which will invite retaliation (Planned Parenthood of Southeastern Pennsylvania v. Robert Casey, Supreme Court of the United States 1992). We gain information about abused wives of homosexual men who demand protection of their "macho" images in the community; wives concealing abusive behavior which might end their husbands' political careers; women who have been denied opportunities for employment or sociability by jealous-jailer husbands; women tempted to commit suicide by men who demean so thoroughly that stability and self-assurance are destroyed; women who secretly murder abusive spouses; those women whose disrupted lives negate "normal" relationships with their children; and such correlative problems as recidivist abusers, the lack of equal access to legal representation by women relegated to "overnight indigency"; deprivation of food, shelter, and clothing; the loss of personal, medical, and government benefits; denial of access to appro-priate and available community services; and the examination of collusion between men (business partners, or political allies, or committee participants) to protect each other in a still male-dominated society.

Domestic abuse is an unusually important form of victimization by one person against another because of the many significant relationships: family lifestyle, religious and cultural background, child-rearing practices, foodways, health issues, teen relationships (in and out of the home), divorce, binuclear families, intergenerational cyclic tendencies, and recidivism. The multi-faceted phenomenon has probably received more recent attention by academics and service-provider professionals than have other "personal" crimes, and yet the direct correlation between domestic abuse and the ever-rising female homeless population is not exemplified in long-term, in-depth studies, especially of single middle-aged women. It is identified as one factor occasionally, usually in general statements and in relation to women with children and/or homeless shelters. For example, New York Govenor Mario Cuomo stated that "It is estimated that battered women constitute 40% of homeless families in shelters" (1988); "Woman abuse is the most common cause of homelessness at Wellspring House shelter in Massachusetts" (Hemminger; 1991); "Battering is a significant cause of the rise in female and family homelessness" (*Los Angeles Times* 1990); "41% of the women willing to respond had lived with battering mates before becoming homeless in Boston" (Morgan 1992); "Domestic violence is the cause of 42% of homeless families in Philadelphia" (Pennsylvania Bar Association 1990); and "More than one-half of homeless women are on the street [in the United States] because they are fleeing domestic violence" ("Hearings" 1990). I believe the dearth of specific research on the interrelationship is due to foci which have become stagnated in traditional (disciplinary) studies as opposed to a focus on what victims are expressing.

Since "domestic violence" accounts for a major segment of the scholarly study of victimization, it is appropriate to discuss the differing foci and methodologies which prevail. Sociologists lean on both qualitative and quantitative methods for defining and exploring the phenomenon of domestic violence. Well Known in their field are Drs. R. Emerson and Russel Dobash. In their book *Violence Against Wives* (1979: 12), the Drs. Dobash provide

> in-depth information about the violence itself and the relationship in which it occurs, as well as an analysis of the society in which wife beating occurs and the cultural beliefs and institutional pratices that contribute to this pattern.

The researchers utilized structured interviews with standardized questions, impressionistic accounts, background knowledge, public records, statements by public officials, and newspaper accounts (1979). While the Dobashes advocate economic, legal, and political equality for women, they stress historical analysis and the association of female subordination to a patriarchal family structure. Other sociologists focus on sexism; men's and women's liberation; and relationship-specific abusiveness within the family setting, such as elder, sibling, or father-child. In general, there exists a plethora of material regarding the historical oppression of women and family dysfunctions and a dearth of information pertaining to specific ethnic/cultural beliefs and behaviors and the consequential effects of domestic abuse.

Psychologists studying abused women and abusers try to determine the whys of particular (hereditary and environmental) behaviors—the shaping and effects of personality traits—and examine types of therapies. Well known for representing the psychological perspective in such matters is the work of feminist psychotherapist Lenore Walker (*The Battered Woman*), who has adopted an informant-centered methodology: "These [battered] women told me how rare it was to tell their entire stories to someone" (1979: xii). Walker's hypotheses concerning battered women, however, are based on the analysis of case-studies of patients able to afford (or otherwise undergo) psychotherapy sessions. Unfortunately, there has been literally no recognition by researchers or scholars that victims' stories are almost always garnered from shelter residents and counseling clients—certainly not groups representative of the wider population, for only a minute percentage of abused women seek counseling, call crisis/shelter hotlines, or enter sanctuaries. Further, women *desiring* shelter residence are screened to fit particular requirements and are at the mercy of available space. "When poor, battered women leave home, they cannot rely on the availability of affordable public housing or shelters. Space in shelters is extremely limited: in 1989 a Los Angeles county grand jury found that 90% of the battered women and children who sought safety were turned away; in Washington D.C. eight in ten women are told there is no room" (*Los Angeles Times* 1990: Pt. Q, 37). Women Against Abuse in Philadelphia (Pennsylvania) report that while they provided 19,000 shelter days during 1990-1991, they had to turn away 1448 adults due to lack of space. According to a New York study, "Getting into a shelter is no guarantee of escaping from the abuse, because most shelters allow only short stays. After being sheltered, 31% of abused women returned to their batterers, primarily because they could not locate longer-term housing" (Dwyer and Tully 1989: 9). In any case, "when a battered woman leaves her abuser, there is a 50% chance that her standard of living will drop below the poverty line" (Hearings; 1990: 95). We gain a clear picture of a most important database that is never heard from: the heretofore non-associated drifting-homeless; suicide attempters who may be institutionalized, closeted with relatives, or finally successful; those women who have committed or have seriously contemplated committing murder to end victim-ization; monied victims who have the ability to quietly divorce and begin a new life; and women who are forced to return to previous lifestyles which rely on parental support.

Literature from the field of social work tends to emphasize characteristics of victims and abusers and provides suggestions for agency policy(ies), while the therapeutic perspectives describe techniques for treatment and rehabilitation of offenders and counseling for battered women. Ramifications include arguments concerning "who is to blame" and resultant foci for treatment. Peter Neidig, for example, has challenged gender-specific intervention measures in favor of *couples*-therapy; he disputes the assumption of male fault, relinquishing the labels of "abuser" and "victim" to a conceptualization of equal-partner blame for battering. He contends that the political activists of the feminist movement have created a biased focus on issues of domestic violence (1984). Immediate responses from those working in the battered women's movement—and from both sexes representing the social work field—challenge Neidig's assumptions and point to the diversity of positions/beliefs among practitioners and researchers involved in treating and eliminating violent behavior. In particular, Ellen Pence (representative of the Minnesota Domestic Abuse Intervention Project) cites not only prevailing literature but current arrest and incarceration practices as evidence that Neidig's commentary ("Men continue to engage in abusive behavior not because they believe it is right but because they lack the skills to do otherwise..."[1984: 473]) is untenable. Her response (1984: 477) evokes vivid imagery:

> Certainly both parties have their story to tell, but one of the people telling the story has a black eye, a cut lip, a swollen face, or smashed teeth and the other does not. It is political to ignore that the gender of the person injured is female.

(Repeatedly we hear reference to the "telling of one's story." It is significant that the *content* alone of a tale is recognized; discussion of the *storytellers* is limited to gender and physical damage.)

It is not surprising that a variety of perspectives and assumptions surface from the proponents of differing disciplines. What *is* suprising is that with all of the bases covered, so to speak, there is still an alarming increase in violence within families (or "domestic situations," since one must acknowledge battering/abuse in homosexual, extended family, and "living-together" relationships as well). Arguments do exist that domestic violence *per se* is not on the rise, but that only the *reporting* of it has increased. That the reporting of abuse is more prevalent is not disputed; however, since, according to the FBI, *all* types of crime showed upswings in all regions of the country, led by violent crimes with an increase by 12% (1987), one would have to present startling evidence to prove that domestic violence is not included in this increase. According to a report-for-the-future written by R. Morton Darrow (head of Darrow Associates, a think tank for managers of business, government, higher education, and non-profit groups) for Family Service America, the umbrella group for the estimated 275 not-for-profit family service agencies in the United States and Canada, fore-casts include the continuous increase of violence within families—and a congruent increase in institutional and agency intervention (1987). In 1993, researchers at the U.S. Centers for Disease Control and Prevention in Atlanta confirm the forecast that there is a growing epidemic of violence against women and assign ten experts to outline plans to launch specific programs aimed at curbing such violence (*Los Angeles Times*, May 24).

Surprising also is the extent to which the *consequences* of battering are limited. In "Adult Domestic Violence: The Law's Response" (1983: 153), Nadine Taub (director of the Women's Rights Litigation Clinic) observes:

> The consequences of allowing battering to continue can be serious: experts believe that domestic violence is likely to escalate in cyclical fashion, at times resulting in the woman's death. Women caught in the cycle of abuse may, in the process of defending themselves, kill their assailants. Children exposed to such patterns of violence may not only suffer immediate emotional distress, but may also reproduce their parents' behavior patterns as adults...The incidence of violence has been associated specifically with alcohol and drug abuse and changes in family circumstances, such as pregnancy.

While the correlations noted by Taub are relatively common themes, in-depth studies focusing on many other consequences of battering are often *expressed* by victims in interviews and case studies, but are seemingly deemed irrelevant by the majority of researchers, e.g., post-trauma physical illness(es), supranormal experiences, food and sleep disorders, disorientation, phobias, victimization by particular individuals/system/state, recidivism, and homelessness (with congruent problems).

The discipline of criminology has contributed the most comprehensive study of the total complex of issues that are involved in dealing with abuse: cultural norms and expectations of society, the legal aspects of criminality, the interaction of all participants in situational context, and rehabilitative and preventative measures. As a result, victimology—the study of the victim and a distinct focus of inquiry within the larger field of criminology—places the individual in an active role in the victim-criminal relationship, and examines the concepts of responsibility, motivations, and behaviors. While personal identity becomes a recognizable element, the approach is still an etic one: victims' experiences and ideas are subordinated to researchers' concepts, labels, and solutions.

Crime-related research has, in the past, focused more on the problems and rights of the offenders than the victims. In recent years, however, a new perspective in victimology attempts to *balance* the preoccupation with identifying and assisting the offenders by addressing the attackers' victims. Unfortunately, there is a risk; Emilio Viano (1983: 22) notes that there is a *new-found* scapegoat to explain criminal behavior: the victim.

> Some criminologists have quickly seized the opportunity to claim that victims of assault have no one else but themselves to blame if they were attacked when walking in a dark alley, or that victims of sexual assault "provoked" the attack by wearing attractive clothes, or by accompanying their acquaintance to a secluded place, or by hitchhiking.

Interestingly, Wachs' study of crime victims' narratives points to a similar perception by the victims themselves: "The overall design of the crime-victim narrative rests on a motif sequence underscored by the theme of the chance encounter; the victims often conclude that they were in the wrong place at the wrong time" (1981:18). In addition, Wachs notes that these stories impart crime prevention skills: a survival code which "emphasizes surrender in the face of the victimization experience" (1981: 27). Wachs bases the code of survival on two folk attitudes: fatalism and misjudgment. It is significant that Wachs' study is of muggings in the city, and Viano's study is in regard to victims generically. The women's movement has adopted the attitude that battered women blame themselves (by virtue of low self-esteem) for abuse by their spouses. It is certainly true that many women do assume that they have "done something wrong" to attract such injurious attention. However, my research has uncovered quite another propensity: to place the blame exactly where it belongs, on the offender and/or the state ("system"). I collected thousands of personal experience narratives from women who were not residents of shelters or missions. Many are living out of cars which are necessarily in hidden places. Some women travel almost continuously in their vans/campers, even if their circuit is a narrow one. Other women spend their days and nights in huge airline terminals or on spreading campuses, moving from one area to another. They are often in social and/or psychological isolation if not actual physical separation, and have had little if no contact. With social service providers or psychologists, and what confidences they tried to share were not valued. Thus, when they finally told me their stories, they reflected a lack of "influence" by personnel who "led" them into discussions of such esoteric matters as cyclic patterning, prior family victimization, and transactional analysis. While I am not castigating the well-meaning feminist and psychoanalytic practitioners, I have to question why so many women who have had *no* contact with such dedicated professionals and workers present detailed and unambiguous scenarios of victimization in which they were plainly at no fault at all. In fact, the more isolated the existence of the victim, the more I heard regarding the guilt of the victimizer (s). Part of this tendency I must adjudge as an ego-enhancer in the face of unbelievably harsh living conditions resulting from enforced (and often long-term) homelessness. Another factor is fear. Women are very aware of how they arrived at a present, undesirable circumstance, and many know that even after leaving their homes and belongings, they are not safe from abusers. In Jones' 1980 study, she cites two cases in which abusers tracked their spouses across state lines for retaliation, and another batterer found his wife seven years after she left and "cut her up." Research over a ten year period indicates that women who leave their abusers are at 75% greater risk of being killed than are those who stay (*NCADV Voice* 1989). When I met with Donna in her cave-like dwelling in the hills of rural Pennsylvania in 1977, she made it quite clear that she took no responsibility for her lack of home and normal life.

> That rat ruined my life by running me out of my house. He kept telling everyone that I made him miserable. So why didn't *he* leave? If I was so stingy with him, then how come *he's* got all our money? I was the generous and loving one, Goddammit! But I don't get to tell anyone. Just look at me. I was never a mess *before*.

I must consider that when a victim is alone and has searched her memory for the rationale which places her where she is, she has repeated many events in her life to herself (in storytelling form) and, more often than has been recognized, concludes that her situation is not as others perceive it—or would have her perceive it.

Viano (1983: 25) addresses the issue of omitted victims, a class in which I place the abused woman rendered homeless:

> Large groups of crimes have been neglected. . . victims of omission and neglect rather than commission, victims that are not *identifiable* individuals but organizations or *classes of people.* In other words, it appears that victimologists have preferred the most common, less controversial, more obvious, more easily applicable definitions of *who the victims are and who may be a victim.* . . the minorities and women, women, the failures of the justice system, the scandals surrounding the treatment of old people, the mentally ill, require that an enlarged list of victims receive the attention of scholars.

Populations are known because researchers have access to them—in shelters, on Skid Rows, from hotline calls, from court appearances, welfare rolls, police reports, etc. There are *no* statistics for women who blend into society either by escaping into another, better life, or who daily disappear from polite society. Viano is concerned with the societal impact, noting the need for "channeling fear, rage, and grief into positive avenues for change, including forging new and stronger community ties" (1983: 29).

An international movement (accredited to English penal reformer Margery Fry in the 1950s) for the recognition of victims as deserving appropriate and public compensation acknowledged the *individual-as-victim* even before the emergent battered women's movement in the 1970s. The individual-as-victim has also taken new meaning; with the criminal justice system under scrutiny, the implication arises of criminality involving more than a relationship between two people: the victim of a criminal may also become a victim of the state (Viano, 1976). This link to a lack of dedication and/or competency and/or inadequacy in regard to the needs of community members has not been explored in the relationship between such lacks and the abused woman driven to involuntary homelessness. While Pence (and other researchers in similar commentary) have stated the goals of the battered women's movement to be eliminating violence against women, utilizing strategies to create and maintain shelters, and holding men accountable by pressuring the legal system to respond to such episodes as violent crimes rather than "domestic conflicts" or "marital spats" (1984: 479), the focus is still on an acknowledgment of "violence"—and a legal response. A report endorsed by the California Attorney General (John Van de Kamp) points to the inaccessibility of the public to the disciplinary procedure of the State Bar Association and a related problem within the Bar itself to uncover incompetent lawyers, referring to the current disciplinary system in analogy to a Rube Goldberg procedure (1987). Monitor Robert Fellmeth, who conducted the investigation, criticized the Bar for neither discovering nor preventing improper behavior of lawyers. In addition, Fellmeth found that only an aggressive and articulate (alleged) victim of an attorney might stand a chance of having his or her case being considered for initial acceptance (1987). This admission of attorney malfeasance and/or nonfeasance is also suggested by the Maryland Court of Appeals in its appointment of a committee to study the American Bar Association Model Rules of Professional Conduct (1983). That committee recommended changes in the standards for ethical conduct for Maryland lawyers (1985), but nothing has changed victims' access to the disciplinary procedure—which is totally within the control of an autonomous unit: the Attorney Grievance Commission (staffed by attorneys). A victim's only alternative is to hire an attorney to try individual cases of malfeasance at the District Court level. That is an impossibility for impoverished and homeless people, especially in light of massive cutbacks in legal aid services. In my work in Maryland and California, I have searched in vain for attorneys who will represent a domestic violence victim in court without any costs. A few states claim volunteer attorneys who offer free services to victims, but the strict rules of compliance negate virtually all victims. For instance, if a woman has been rendered homeless and has had to move out of the area, she would have to return to the state in which the abuse occurred to work with the volunteer attorney. Where will she stay? Who will feed her, give her transportation money, and provide proper clothing and other necessities while she awaits what is always a lengthy procedure? Not the attorney—or any agency. And so the promise of legal assistance to every domestic violence victim is a hollow one.

There is an assumption among most Americans that "justice" is affected by the professionals who work *for* the victim in the court system. Taub's commentary (1983: 156) reflects what others in the legal system know but are loathe to admit:

> Prosecutors may likewise share society's general attitude that domestic violence should not be considered criminal. there may also be structural constraints on the ability of prosecutors' offices to respond to the demands that would result from reducing police discretion to avoid arrest. Geared more toward the sensational crimes that are often related to political and career advancement, such offices may simply not make the necessary resources available.

The 10 January 1895 issue of the *Sacramento Bee* reports a ruling which has altered the manner in which police respond to certain domestic violence situations. Judge James T. Ford found in a battered woman's favor in a lawsuit against a sheriff's department and individual officers, ruling that a police officer has a duty to act against a person who has violated a restraining order issued by the court. Batterers have traditionally utilized the excuse that they cannot be held responsible for actions against a spouse because they were *admitted* to the house from which they were barred—and officers have deferred to the batterer. The victim's attorney commented that the new ruling has taken one weapon away from the abuser. Unfortunately, victims' stories tell us of many more.

There is also an assumption by most Americans that community services loudly and proudly proclaimed to assist victims exist and effectively pursue "justice." Maryland, for example, has a multitude of community services designed to prevent victimization of women. Personal experience narratives provide undeniable evidence that many of these services either do not exist or do not provide the assistance promised. There need be no inferences that collusion and corruption occur to create homeless women; absolute proof can be provided in the offenders' own signatures on official stationry or court form. The victims who are anxious to show such evidence to those in authority are rarely successful; they are limited to telling their stories to whomever will listen—usually other victims.

While international symposia have been devoted to victimology since 1973, there have been no direct correlations between victims of domestic abuse and the rising female-homeless population. Investigation is circumventing these issues, even though victims express such correlatives. Why? The feminist perspective, which is almost entirely responsible for the un-yielding attention to victims of domestic abuse, has been circumspect in its foci, stressing the characteristics of and reasons for care systems while avoiding direct confrontation of issues which embarrass funding sources and politicians. In addition, the women's movement appears to be totally *committed* to Lenore Walker's concepts of "learned helplessness" and "cyclic batter-ing syndrome" (1979). As an example of such commitment, a *Skills for Violence-Free Relationships* "textbook" (written by Barrie Levy for the Southern California Coalition on Battered Women) is utilized in classrooms throughout the country. This book presents information and activities designed to promote understanding of the situations and behaviors of domestic violence. Instructions to the teacher include: "As you conclude discussion [of battering relationships] emphasize the point that the cycle of violence happens over and over again, sometimes every day or week, and in some families much less often. *The cycle of violence happens in all battering relationships*" (1985: 47). On the basis of my own interviews with victims, and statements made by victims (under oath) in court, I can state emphatically that this contention is simply not tenable. These concepts—"learned helplessness" and "cyclic battering syn-drome"—*may* occur, but certainly not in *all* cases of domestic abuse. And they refer to *battering*, not to psychological abuse, which is invariably continuous over an extended period. The unfortunate implication of such "theories" (and resultant "textbooks") is that females all behave in the same manner and males all behave in the same manner—and they react to each other in the same manner.

The attempt to conceptualize victimization involves, almost inevitably, typifications. As specialists formulate definitions and adduce examples, they tend to create types or categories. The danger lies in misunderstanding and/or omission: one may self-identify as a victim but either express oneself poorly or be perceived improperly and thereby be typified incorrectly. Conceptualizing victimization involves the perceptions of four distinct entities: the individual (the victim and any relevant other[s]), the abuser, society-at-large, and the researcher. The victim—for the purpose of this discussion an abused wife/homeless person—is in a unique position in society. She is in marginal circumstances. It is therefore necessary to examine the nature of a marginal existence.

Victor Turner, in expanding on the nature and characteristics of Arnold van Gennep's (1909) term"liminal phase," distinguishes between a stable state and a transitional period. The victim and the process of victimization may be perceived as within "transition," in which van Gennep's three phases—separation, *limen*, and aggregation—occur: 1)the victim is symbolically detached from "an earlier fixed point in the social structure and from a set of cultural conditions," 2) "the passenger" passes through a cultural realm that is distinct from the past or forthcoming stable state, and 3) the victim—the ritual individual—becomes a part of a structuralized state in which behavior and a social position are recognized, and rights and obligations are expected (1969: 94).

Turner notes that those in liminality are 1) persons who fall into the interstices of social structure, 2) persons on the margins of the social structure, or 3) those who occupy the lowest rungs of the social structure (1969: 125). The homeless are certainly liminal beings in all senses. Victims of domestic abuse may be symbolically marginal, covertly displaced in mind only, or overtly homeless. "Threshold people" in this transitional or liminal phase of life may be undergoing a process which is "betwixt and between the categories of ordinary social life" (1974: 53); the attribute of liminality is analogous to one of visible-invisibility-in-society. Many abused and nearly all homeless individuals are defrocked of status privileges, property, and rights. They then share the same "nothingness" as others similarly and symbolically dehumanized, and are forced to tailor coping mechanisms which fit their new societal circumstances. These formulated mechanisms consist of more than individual creations; they are social frames of references which mold tie-bondings between individuals in transition. Turner has labeled such tie-bondings "communitas" (1974: 53):

> The bonds of communitas are antistructural in the sense that they are undifferentiated, equalitarian, direct, non-rational (though not irrational), I-Thou relationships. In the liminal phase [of rites] communitas is engendered by ritual humiliation, stripping of signs and insignia of preliminal status, ritual leveling, and ordeals and tests of various kinds intended to show that 'man thou art dust!'

Principals in the throes of liminality may cope by creating a bonding communitas. One does not have to be an initiate in any formal ceremonial process; the concept is applicable to victims who share a mental or physical degradation which society members impose. "Normal" social relationships are transcended; victims have experienced the extraordinary and share a bonding which draws upon the constraints imposed by societal structure and ordeals that have humiliated beyond others' comprehension. Battered women may find communitas in a temporary shelter which caters to their particular needs while communitas among the homeless takes on the "immediacy of the moment," dealing with experiences spontaneously and without regard to approval or acceptability by societal standards. The "Love Camp," a conglomerate of tent and carton dwellers in Los Angeles' Skid Row section, just "appeared" (as several have done since 1984) in response to the human desire for companionship-of-a-like-kind. The residents support each other in the most basic of ways, working in a commune fashion with each resident assuming chores. Maury Greene expresses their camp thusly: "All we want is a chance to be together and support each other" (1987). As the police "swept" downtown streets of homeless men and women in February (of 1987), Dave Bryant (of Love Camp) told a television newsman: "We want to stay together as a family and we can't be sure we'll all find space together again as a family." Their concern was not that they were being forced to move from a certain spot; a "brotherhood" had developed among individuals who shared a liminal phase and its leveling influence. The feelings of togetherness would not have occurred in their prior disparate lives. The process of losing status and now sharing hardships in societal "disgrace" created the bond. Eddie (from Love Camp, 1987) says:

> You don't get here from nowhere, man. It's a long road, you can bet, but it ain't that hard. It's a real easy slide down a hill, but that damn hill is studded with nails, and you get stabbed and torn by every one of them. We all know that here. We all come down that hill, maybe not together, but it's all the same thing, and we all are here now; we're all together now, man. We need each other, man. We're all that we got, and we understand each other. Just let us hang together.

Dave and Eddie tell us that each person in Love Camp is important; each contributes something worthwhile to the group. It can be stated that individual members have a stake in the future of Love Camp, i.e., they are stakeholders in the unit which they created and maintain with effort on a daily basis. The tiny community is recognizable as an entity; communitas is expressed through the spoken word and acts of mutual benefit. The residents have come to depend on each other, and the threat of the loss of that bonding is psychologically harmful. In fact, the loss is not one couched only in terms of particular individuals, but of the community itself. It is ironic, perhaps, that contemporary law should define and exemplify that which "community" and "communitas" are. In a landmark case involving the loss not only of lives but of a community, the United States District Court held for the surviving residents of Buffalo Creek (a West Virginia coal mining town which disappeared in a flood caused by the negligence of the dam operators). Gerald Stern, one of the attorneys for the plaintiffs, explains the rationale (1976: 301):

> We coined the term 'psychic impairment' to include both the psychiatric damages identified by Dr. Lifton and the loss of communality found by Dr. Erikson. . . .We insisted that all of the survivors were entitled to recover for their mental suffering, even if they suffered no physical injury, saw or heard no relative or friend in peril, or were absent from the valley on the day of the disaster. We argued that each resident of the valley, even those who were not there during the flood, was a direct victim of the coal company's reckless conduct and not merely a bystander. . . . The court was persuaded that the relief provided by the law should be determined not by narrow traditional legal principles but by fairly modern psychiatric and sociological principles.

The decision of this court is thus one that recognizes communitas as a concept of human relationships that are inherent in such communities as Love Camp, Buffalo Creek, and others in which fellowship, sociability, and dependency are exhibited. It is not unusual for these communities to be populated by individuals who are isolated geographically or occupationally. I suggest that the characteristics of community and communitas may be found among the victims of homelessness precisely because of their isolation from the larger society. It is very apparent in the occasional enclave of vans, campers, and motorhomes that are usually lined-up adjacent to large parcels of almost-vacant urban land that is undergoing slow and long-term construction and in rural areas, especially in hilly countryside, where a grouping may be quite close or spread out over a few acres.

The perception of communitas among the homeless is expressed above all in the process of storytelling, through which communal attitudes are identified and reinforced. Teddy has a repertoire of stories about his and his friends' current (1987) lifestyle.

> Hey! Keep off my turf. Whatcha mean, it's the city's? I *been* here! I *be* here! Two years now. That's my corner. And that's my cartons. And you know where *my* place in line is. And *my* place at the table. Sam here is behind me. So let's keep it like it was and it is, OK? Get your own act together, sucker, or you'll answer to me and my pals. We earned what we got and we'll get more, see? We all got something to say and there's going to be more people to listen. Let me tell you how Harry over there got his new tent.

This type of camaraderie acts both as support system and as an incentive for action. The purchasing of tents was generated by Teddy's stories of one man's success. A grouping of such tents developed on a (Los Angeles) vacant lot, and the dwellers formed a unit with elected leaders, voluntary and assigned chores, and a recognized status ranking. A small society was created. Thus, communitas which is born in liminality may be expanded—but as Turner has indicated (1974: 169) it is also distinct from a "structured" group which organizes because of an original *utilitarian* purpose:

> Normative communitas, where under the influence of time, the need to mobilize and organize resources to keep the members of a group alive and thriving, and the necessity for social control among those members in pursuance of these and other collective goals. . . begins with a nonutilitarian experience of brotherhood and fellowship the form of which the resulting group tried to preserve, in and by its religious and ethical codes and legal and political statutes and regulations.

The strategies for positive action by Teddy, Harry, and others to preserve fellowship and brotherhood were formed to acknowledge symbolically the liminal phase, exercise control over the situation, and effect changes in the marginality. Liminality is, then, the root of old identification and the birthplace of new identity. Identity as a victim does not disappear, but may simply change focus—perhaps in the name of "justice." One of the tent communities that the homeless founded in downtown Los Angeles is called Justiceville.

As a concept, "homelessness" defies definitive agreement even in the 1990s. The general public tends to designate anyone without a "permanent home" (rented room, apartment, trailer, or house) as homeless. Researchers in varied fields, however, argue over aspects of "chronic" or "episodic" homelessness, trying to distinguish how many *days a month* an individual might live in a hotel/shelter/mission before he or she can be labeled "homeless." Studies by various governmental and private agencies periodically claim knowledge of the number of homeless in any given city, but figures vary so drastically that one realizes that there is no way to count a population which drifts and hides. We cannot ascertain whether numbers are not sometimes increased in an attempt to cull more dollars from funding sources or if the numbers are not underestimated due to the invisible homeless who sleep in all-night theaters, airline terminals, cars, warehouses, and on beaches. It is not disputed, however, that there is an alarming rise in the numbers of homeless people. On April 29, 1986 the U.S. Conference of Mayors released information to the news media on the disturbing trend in the growing number of families with children seeking emergency shelter. In conjunction with that report, Robert G. Vilmur of the Los Angeles Human Services Division characterized the city's three main types of homeless: the chronically disabled (e.g., alcoholics), those who have lost their jobs, and individuals traumatized by home events who may have run away (1986). The latter category suggest teenagers; it certainly does not tell us anything about the older women we see pushing carts filled with their belongings.

Obviously there is a need for more extensive and intensive research pertaining to the correlation between women leaving abusive relationships and the phenomenon of homelessness. The typification of the homeless person as a Skid Row or shelter dweller, an alcohol or drug user, poorly educated, and/or as mentally ill or minority leads to unfortunate and improper assumptions about and prevents effective solutions to the problem(s). Women are lumped into categories that were meant for an all-male population. These typifications also lead us to the discouraging assumption that this entire population is not ever going to be able to fit into "our" society: they are deemed either voluntarily unwilling to work or involuntarily "weak." If, however, one pays heed to that which homeless individuals, and especially homeless women are saying, then it is apparent that there is a large population of victims who can easily escape homelessness before it becomes a permanent state. Some feminists engaged in urban planning have recognized the link between domesticity and housing. In particular, Jacqueline Leavitt and Susan Saegert have conducted research into the effectiveness of co-op living "as models of human survival in which housing plays a part" and in which "stereotypes of the dependent poor" are negated (1984: 32, 37). Leavitt and Saegert (1984: 37)

> listened to the stories of women who provide models for a feminism actively committed to social justice. . . [and] models for aging in which the elders use their knowledge of human life as well as the skills and relationships built up over a lifetime to pass on a vision of community.

Leavitt and Saegert point out the need for abandoning our stereotypes of "poor" women and their ability to mobilize in the community as a part of a larger ethical issue. We must recognize the inalienable right human beings have to basic necessities (food, shelter, and clothing), and then in what order these will be provided. Nationally recognized advocate for the homeless, Mitch Snyder, taught us a valuable lesson when he walked off of a talk show because there was an argument among several prominent civic leaders regarding the number of homeless people in the country. Why did it matter if there were one million or five million? All we need to address is the issue of human suffering in untenable quantity. It is within this scope that I address the situations and behaviors which create and attend abuse, deception, and homelessness. The victim becomes the pivotal point in the interrelated societal problems; her self-image and self-described abilities demand solutions.

Eighteen years of personal contact with and direct services to individuals in crisis and post-crisis situations have led me to the following observations and insights concerning self-image and identification as related to victimization: 1) there are individuals who identify themselves immediately as a "victim" relating expansive details of the scenario(s) leading to and perpetuating victimization; 2) there are individuals who tell a tale to an audience about circumstances which are clearly a process of victimization, but who do not identify as a "victim," assuming that what has happened is either their fault (with guilt or embarrassment to be concealed) or an act of fate or God; and 3) there are those who express prior victimization, but reject a current identity as "victim" considering the label negative to their self-image, and insist that they are "survivors," albeit (perhaps unwittingly) revealing through storytelling a *permanent* loss of specific rights, opportunities, and benefits (personal, social, medical, government)—in other words, expressing quite the opposite of the "I-have-overcome" survivor-identity.

A common phrase among victims of abuse is "I am (was) not a person anymore." If one feels like a "victim," one identifies accordingly, and that identification is acted out in various ways: idionarrating, storytelling to others, poetry written or spoken, the supranormal experienced, activist (e)motions, psychological depression, or physical illness. Storytelling to oneself or to others is probably the most common mode of communication among victims, for it is not only catharsis, but is a catalyst for activity: fighting back, forming grassroots organizations, picketing, etc. Self and personhood may accept victimization, often by losing interest in life altogether, or retaliate by an "attack" mode. The "get-on-with-life" attitude is often responsible for one's purposive identification as a "survivor" as opposed to "victim," although there is much debate over these labels. Among grassroots organizations which prefer to call their members "victims," and their groups "victims' rights" organizations, there are pressing problems of providing continuing services as well as advocating for legislative changes in disputable systems, e.g., the criminal justice system.

A positive self-image does not mean that a person cannot and does not identify as a "victim," for in its larger sense

everyone *alive* is a "survivor." One can see an analogous situation among Holocaust "survivors" who perceive "life" as the
important factor; surviving to them means not merely not having
died but, more importantly, being alive to tell about one's
experiences. These survivors express victimization not just as a
temporary (liminal) condition, but in terms of permanent and
continuing damage to body and/or soul, i.e., to their
personhood. They seek *indemnification* as opposed to the more
commonly noted form of restitution: compensation. (Indemnification implies that a future must be provided for rather than
just a past for which to be compensated.)

The crucial question is not that of survival, it is rather one
of human worth and human dignity, and above all, that which
Albert Jonsen calls "personhood" (1987: 3):

> We talk about the maintenance of life; we rarely talk about
> the maintenance of personhood. It is of very little interest
> to me to be alive as an organism. In such a state, I have no
> interests literally. It is enormously interesting for me to be
> a person, with my history, with my place in life, doing the
> things I enjoy doing, loving those I love, causing the
> problems I like to cause. I live my life. It is the
> perpetuation of my personhood that interests me.

Our expressions of perpetuation of personhood are communicated most often in personal experience narratives. In the next
chapter I will discuss the significance of the process of storytelling to oneself about the concerns of personhood.

CHAPTER TWO

"I've Never Told My Story to Anyone Before": Idionarrating & Life Events in Introspect and Retrospect

Barbara Myerhoff states (1980: 30):

> In humans, language is in the higher functions of the neocortex. Neuro-biologists and linguists are beginning to suggest that language is more important for telling stories than it is for directing action. In other words, we must tell stories; it can be said we are designed biologically to do so.

Folklorists have long studied storytelling, that mode of communication in which individuals express their attitudes concerning what they believe to be true and fictive happenings, and which may unconsciously or consciously reveal the effects of tradition and culture. What folklorists have examined are the situations and behaviors of storytellings *between individuals*. What they have not studied is the expressiveness which occurs within one's mind as self-to-self communicating in the narrative form. I will explore a concept which I have termed idionarrating (and idionarrative).

Idionarrating is a reminiscence of an experience which is communicated internally between self-as-teller and self-as-audience. It is in its strictest sense the truly *personal* experience narrative. Self has been involved in the experience and is, in effect, giving part of "its self" in the characterization of the event. In essence, self becomes the ultimate soul-mate with which to commune. Self provides fellowship or sociability when there may be no others to share in a personal moment and where feedback is often needed. (I will refer occasionally to fellowship *and/or* sociability. I find a subtle difference: fellowship may be

27

the condition of finding oneself in the company of others of compatible nature, while sociability connotes an act of participation with those others.)

Just as it is quite natural for human beings to narrate to others, it is natural for them to communicate ideas and feelings to themselves. We take for granted "self-talk"; we walk the stores, streets, and workplace silently comparing, contrasting, and commenting. There is also, however, adequate evidence of idionarrating: we recall the past and in the process of reminiscing re-live a prior experience for the purpose of self-indulgence (in the positive sense of the term). What begins as a personal adventure in reviving mental impressions may be shared with others, but reminiscing may also be a completely private act.

We daydream in a narrative mode, and daydreaming plays a significant role in life; it is a way to imagine what could have been or what still might be. While subsequent action is often the result of a daydream, it is not necessary. Such silent storytelling is "self" narrating to "self" and in this sense is a self-indulgence. We also know that human beings make up stories. People invent excuses, explanations, and entertaining events in story format. We are creative, then, in a narrative mode for any number of reasons during our waking hours. In addition, Norman Cameron postulates that we are also creative in our sleep: "Dreams are strange forms of personal artistic creation, plays which provide their own stage and their own scenery" (1963: 15).

It can be postulated that the act of storytelling is also an act of maintenance of our own personhood: a performance which is deliberately meant to let ourselves and others know how we feel about life in particular and in general. A meta-reality is created during narrating. This concrete construct permits one to address that which may be elusive and difficult to deal with. Narratives which are personal in nature contain the most intimate information which we can impart. Therefore sharing is usually a selective procedure. An embarrassing victimization, for instance, will not be shared as easily as a story about a misplaced shoe. What happens when the memory of a particularly traumatic experience to self flashes through one's mind and self decides that the story cannot be told to any other person? Because we are inherently storytellers, our brains will function despite the reluctance of the will. If we are biologically coded to tell *stories*, that implies that our brain already "knows" how to pattern or sequence, for a *story* entails structuring selected elements of reality into a meaningful sequence as opposed to a total disregard for intelligibility. However, as part of the socialization process which begins in infancy, we progressively learn how to structure our stories in the manner in which others in our society expect them to be told and heard. The process of reconstructing an experience consists of utilizing the characters and actions in their proper places and to their best advantage. The creative aspects of story telling are also satisfied, e.g., selecting the proper words to evoke just the right image, even if self is the only audience. Patty (age 44, Santa Monica, California, 1984) reflects on her life:

> When the sound of his voice fills my head and I can taste the blood, I'll just take a pillow into the closet, cover myself with coats, and scream into the pillow that I hate him and want him to die an awful death. I'll scream until I don't feel like it will happen again, but I can remember each time that he's pretended that it would be a normal evening and it won't end up with me on the floor. I've never even told the paramedics; I've had to lie. He'd have killed me for sure if I'd told anyone what he does to me. But I know. I can't get it out of my mind. My head gets filled with what happened and I start to think about it like a book. A script really. I'll go over every bit of what happened as if it were a movie script and I was the actress. I know all the lines, and if just one little thing isn't quite right, I'll start over again and do it just the way it happened. I'm in rehearsal, and if the scene is right on, then I pretend I'm allowed to change the script to how it would be the next time so I won't be hurt. I know so many scripts by heart. I've memorized them and I go over and over them. Then I need to scream to make up for not telling anyone. I can only tell me and the pillow. I once had the feeling that the pillow could really hear me. It was filled more with my spirit and life than it was with feathers. I'd go mad without that closet. It's my lifeline.

"If no one listened, nevertheless the tale is told, aloud, to oneself, to prove that there is existence, to tame the chaos of the world, to give meaning. The tale certifies the fact of being and gives sense at the same time" (Myerhoff 1980: 30). The tale may be told in silence to oneself before it is told aloud to oneself because the mind simply cannot rid itself of the experience. Only in amnesia does the event seem to disappear from memory—and then, apparently, it is only in hiding. The rest of our experiences can be coaxed into remembrance by just the right sensory stimulus or connecting thought, even though there are many we would like to forget.

When the brain is activated into recall and an experience is re-lived, we must arrive at the conclusion that the actual process of narrating begins with memory: the ability to revive images from the past. The derivation of "memory" indicates remembering, from the Latin *memor*, and the act of remembrance: the process of past experiences/events coming to mind again. Following that memory or remembrance, "reminiscence" (from the Latin *reminiscens*) connotes not only the memory of an experience, but the accounting of same through language (which may be written or spoken aloud or silent). "Memoir," derived from (French and) Latin, is also *memoria*: memory, while *memorabilis* (Latin) denotes "e.g., memorable things worth remembering; notable; or remarkable." Thus the *ability* to revive a past image innately enables the *process* of reminiscence in silent, oral, or written form. And the key to *what* is revived, remembered, and recounted is its memorability—its noteworthiness. As memory imprints surface and are processed cognitively (accompanied by one's physiological and psychological responses), language and inherent and learned models combine to create "stories." Because sensory stimuli and thought processes may occur in *isolation* (away from other people) there is no reason why a story must be told in interactive communication between *individuals*.. The story may be told to oneself. In fact, the story may *have* to be told solely to oneself; it may necessarily be "a secret." Our biological coding being intact, we narrate to ourselves. Often idionarrating is a deliberate prelude to sharing the experience with others; a secret may be only a temporary one, or specific information may be harbored awaiting revelation at a later date, perhaps for social or political purposes.

The act of narrating is, in part, cathartic. Telling a story may provide pleasure or release tension. In *Number Our Days* (1978) and later articles and conversations, Barbara Myerhoff tells us about the many individuals who survived the Holocaust cherishing a repertoire of stories which they insist is their only reason for living: "They return from hell to bear witness. . . It barely mattered if there was someone listening" (1980: 29). She quotes from a victim of Auschwitz: "[A man] tells people how he lived and died. If nothing else is left, one must scream. Silence is the real crime against humanity" (1980: 29). Consequently, one important purpose of a storytelling that can be articulated is the working through of a personal and/or social crusade. We can reasonably assume that the Holocaust victims went over and over stories of atrocities in their own minds before they "returned from hell." Pent-up emotions—especially fury, despair, and frustration—are vented through storytelling, and similar feelings are expressed by victims of all personal crimes. Telling one's story does indeed validate one's existence and justify life itself. Sandi (age 29, Hermosa Beach, California, 1985) describes her experiences:

> Every night for five years I held my breath and waited for the smash of his fist or the foul words that bounced off the walls like I did. Thank God I am out of it now, even if I don't have a place to live. I had to bottle up all of the things that happened and tell *me* how he tied me up and practiced all that filthy stuff he'd see in dirty movies. No one would have believed me then, and if no one believes me now it isn't because I'm not trying hard to get them to. It's like, if I just keep on telling it, it will make up for all the pain and time we lost. Maybe it makes me feel whole again. I'm a person now, even with all the problems we've got. But I feel really strange sometimes. I find myself telling people I don't know in the grocery store what I been through. They must think I'm really weird, but it sure makes me feel better.

To be a victim is a psycho-physiological experience which calls for coping and cathartic mechanisms. One such mechanism is the structuring of significant details into a narrative form that provides a means of coping. In regard to crime-victim experiences, Wachs notes that "the victim may repeatedly narrate an account of the event to other victims, friends, acquaintances, co-workers, and other available audiences" (1981: 17). Wachs quotes sociologists Robert Lejeune and Nicholas Alex: "The victim often repeats details of the crime experience to any immediate audience." Wachs continues: "Feeling a great psychological need to impart a brush with death, the victims begin to reassert their survival instinct. Having undergone a frightening experience, the victim has lived to tell about it" (1981: 19). Many victims also exhibit an *obsessive* need to convey dismay, horror, fear, guilt, anger, or sadness. Verna (Culver City, California, 1986) was embarrassed:

> I can't believe that I've told you guys this story before! [Laughter from an audience of four.] How many times? [Conflicting responses, laughter, and then commentary by the audience.] Oh, Jeez, I'm embarrassed! So what can I do? It's always on my mind as if it's the only thing on my mind and I've got to get it out right now. I'm sorry! But it's making my knees jerk, it's so strong in my mind. I guess not being able to tell anyone for so long has got me going like a stuck gas peddle! Did I tell you about the night Ken tore out the 30-foot telephone cord and made a fancy noose and hung it from the shower and played with it while he said I was going to be found in the morning with it around my neck? [She had told this story at least ten times within a week.]

But what of the victim who has such a feeling of guilt or shame or fear that she cannot tell anyone of the incident? What happens to that obsessive need to tell? Reggie (age 22, Redondo Beach, California, 1986) had a frightening experience:

> I was knitting and trying to just blank out all of the awful things that were happening by concentrating on counting the stitches, and out of the corner of my eye I saw a light in the closet. That's dumb. It made me look over there, and there was my husband sort of filling the doorway. I stared at him and the light picked up his hair and he glowed and the hair seemed to move first, but he began to come toward me, head first. Like a bull charging. This glowing head was all out of shape, but I knew it was

him. I couldn't move I was so scared. The head got right up to me and then this whole huge body was attached and leaped on me. I fell backwards in the chair and it seemed to be clutching at my chest, gripping me until I couldn't breathe at all. There was this noise, like he was gasping, but I think it was me. And I could smell him. He stunk. I felt like I was going to throw up and all of a sudden the light went out and he disappeared. I was so sick to my stomach and my ribs hurt. For a couple of hours I must have sat there wondering what happened to me. My kid asked me what made me look so bad and I couldn't tell her. What was I going to say? Your father's in Cleveland, but he just came in through the closet and tried to kill me? I don't know how many times I've gone over what happened. I keep trying to see if there was something I missed, but it always comes out the same. That's a horror story, and I can't stop going over it again and again like a stuck record. My brain goes round and round with it. It can't stop playing it, like you've *got* to hear it so many times. But I never told anyone before. He kept telling everyone I was nuts, and for sure they'd believe him if I ever let anyone know what I'd swear happened in that living room.

To the victim who has been living with a traumatic secret, this need to repeat the details of the crime experience is fulfilled *before* another person becomes involved; the story is told to the first immediate audience available: self. Such initial release from extraordinary emotion is necessary to lessen the shock; each telling gives the experience some sense of proportion even if the matter is never resolved. The incident almost becomes acceptable as part of one's repertoire of experiences. Reggie's encounter with a supranormal being was not one she could tell to anyone because she feared being considered crazy. In her case she was already in danger of losing custody of her child. That did not negate her need to relate what happened. She simply kept telling herself the story, and that was not only cathartic, it was therapeutic: she was finally able to come to terms with a problem she had been repressing (see Chapter III).

The notion that psychological release is obtained during solitary aesthetic expression has been explored by Michael Owen Jones in his study of the imprint of grief, discontent, and identifications on a woodworker's creations (1975), and by Edward Ives' observations of unrest, personal loss, and retrospection on a songmaker's repertoire (1978). Designing and lyricism are *internalized* creative processes similar to the reconstructing, rehearsing, and characterizing of a haunting or impressing event; psychological release is obtained by channeling covert distress to overt and symbolic expressiveness—just as significantly (but perhaps not in the same degree) during "silent" storytelling as in narration to others. In vivid imagery and consequent recaptured emotions we respond physiologically; our blood pressures rise and our pulses race while we creatively enjoy, or justify actions while we question, or punish ourselves, or punish others whom we cannot otherwise reach except by *internally* screaming their guilt.

Any scholars may ask how this process is similar to or different from narrating to another individual. Further, he may question how *self*-narrating can contribute to our understanding of narrating as a process and of mankind. In addition, might these insights affect others in some meaningful way?

There are significant distinctions between self-narrating (idionarrating) and narrating amid people. The most obvious, perhaps, is that there need be no "entrance" into a storytelling event. Robert A. Georges has provided us with insights into the nature of storytellings, including the manner in which an event is generated between teller and listeners (1969: 324):

> The structure or the content of the message of an individual storytelling event may be socially prescribed as a result of 1) the nature of the social tensions giving rise to that storytelling event, and 2) the nature of the network of identity relationships and status relationships conceived to exist. . . . The total message of any given storytelling event is generated and shaped by and exists because of a specific storyteller and specific story listeners whose interactions constitute a network of social interrelationships that is unique to that particular storytelling event.

The only socially prescribed rules is idionarrating are those between self and self—two role-players with the same multiple identities of personhood. The storytelling does not depend upon any other social amenities, such as the immediate conversational context and interactions of others (Allen 1978). When the psyche is moved by the unconscious need to narrate, one responds to that need. The self is always there as a receptive audience. If the self as auditor intervenes in the storytelling, it is with some personal correction, addition, or stylistic device which need not be taken negatively as a potential threat to teller's story, but merely as positive feedback which will encourage teller to continue with a "better version."

Psychologically, one "self" in self-narrating performs as alter ego, and all opportunities for raising self-esteem (or denigrating self) and establishing personal identity become operative. Idionarrating is a common and healthy coping mechanism, since one can justify and validate one's feelings or actions with no reprobation except as self dictates. Wish fulfillment is granted until alter ego intercedes. With no "wait" for verbal or nonverbal cues to perform, idionarrating allows free expression.

Another distinction between self-narrating and narrating between individuals is in the way in which feedback and response occur (Georges 1979). As noted above, it does happen between self-teller and self-audience, but self is much kinder than a non-self audience. One can hardly take offense at one's own personal feedback; it is either responded to as positive and helpful or rejected as a "bad idea." Self-audience is truly critical, but always for the betterment of self-teller. Unless one has a psychological need to fail or be denigrated, one only fine-tunes one's stylizing and performance, and self-audience will assist in composing, rehearsing, restructuring, aesthetically up-grading, and cognitively judging without disapproval (or at least without malice).

There are no inferences regarding others' opinions, expectations, or the appropriateness of the story. Self-audience "understands." One can "commune" without fear. The unique personality, style, past, and needs of the teller are innately accepted by self-audience. There need be no opening or closing formulaic markers unless teller's style so dictates. Teller may "jump" into a story, knowing that self-audience is well-aware of dates, locations, and identifying information. On the other hand, self-audience may critique that performance as "lacking," and teller may perceive the advantage of pursuing more comprehensive data to enhance the story. Enhancement is a natural part of creating an interesting characterization of an experience. There is, however, a limit to the kind and amount of embellishment that a *non*-self audience will accept before judging the story to be a tall tale. The self-audience, on the other hand, knows the truth from the beginning; it assesses the narrative regarding its credibility more on whether *others* will accept it rather than on whether the truth is stretched. The self-audience readily desires the teller to continue, and the personal nature of the story may necessitate a graceful excuse, a denial, or an accusation. We acknowledge our own failings and accept them, whereas a non-self audience would judge us differently; we understand *why* we have to tell a story in a particular way.

The teller has much more control over a self-audience. Since self-audience understands exactly what teller is trying to express, self-audience any provide continual positive feedback cues, while a non-self audience may become bored or annoyed and attempt to terminate the storytelling (Georges 1979). Negative feedback by self-audience actually becomes strategy for positive change. This is particularly important to individuals who, like the Holocaust survivors studied by Myerhoff, *must* tell their stories. We all, however, feel at times that we have a story that people should hear, and as folklorists have often noted, we may never receive the opportunity to do so (Allen 1978; Georges 1979; Bard 1986).

While it is hardly possible to tell a story verbatim, time after time, to other people (Georges 1969), it is significant that teller may attempt to do so with self-audience. Each word may have been rehearsed to present a very precise picture of a happening. This is most likely when a traumatic experience is necessarily kept secret. The *details* are listed almost in rote manner; exactness is most important, as any embellishment detracts from the serious and pointed nature of the telling. Self-audience knows this and attempts no changes. If teller strays, self-audience may return teller back to the "correct story": evaluation and judgmental criticism are utilized by "self" for "self" from "self."

Narrators seek out the optimal situations for presenting stories. Time, location, climate, mood, noise, feelings—all may be effective hindrances or incentives to narrating. With self as audience, teller may be able to circumvent any or all variables which a non-self audience responds to; it only matters to *self*-audience how *teller*-self is performing. Since feedback is dependent upon audience perception of teller (and expectations involved), the audience-self at worst is familiar with and empathetic to teller's characterization of an experience.

How, then, is self-narrating indicative of significant insights into man's needs, desires, and planning processes? If *homo. sapiens* is truly *homo narrans*, we are biologically programmed to tell stories. That takes as a given that some human interaction has occasioned the necessity for language and symbols, and that we use our communication ability for particular purposes. Consequently, even when we are alone or unable to share our thoughts, there is fulfillment. The luminescent portraiture and intense feelings which may accompany revived and reconstructed experiences do not wither and retreat into the brain's memory-storage just because there is no one to whom the story can be told; we tell it to ourselves. We may rehearse it just as a play is rehearsed for a performance-to-come so that it is at its optimal form for a storytelling to others.

Consider the "secret story" based upon a traumatic incident. According to a study by Irene Hanson Frieze, 54% of the women reported that they told no one after the first incident of violence. About one-half of the women also said that afterward they tried to comply with the wishes of their husbands. This suggests an attempt to control the battering (1987: 5). As a coping mechanism, such inward communicating and outward activity may be a lengthy one. But victims of rape, near-murder, incest, beatings, or any self and/or societal-labeled "shameful" act constantly refer, finally, to a significant other to "the stories which I could not tell." Jennie reflects on her "self" (1984):

> The "me" of the person people know as Jennie Davidson has been just sort of shriveled-up. People said I was introverted, and I don't know what that means except that I kept to myself. Oh, I mean that I didn't go around telling everyone about all my troubles the way everyone else seems to do. No, I couldn't tell anyone what was happening at home; it was too awful—you know—

embarrassing. But I'd go over and over everything that happened, so I never felt like I hadn't told anyone about the—stuff. And then one day I just decided that I was going to burst, and I said out loud to myself, "I'm going to tell."

The development of one's personal identity is based in part on one's perception of oneself—one's roles as any number of multiple identities—which comprise self-image and sense-of-self. We do not live in isolation, and therefore others intersect our lives; we interact, and we communicate our feelings and attitudes. Then others perceive us, and we recognize that fact, wondering *how* we are perceived as we think about how we perceive other(s). Now we consider how we *desire* to be perceived, and society is acknowledged as an important factor in self-image and sense-of-self. The stories that one tells can never be told exactly as "I" tell them; they are as idiosyncratic as one's never-to-be-duplicated handwriting (idiograph), or one's peculiar speech patterns (idioms and idiolect, or idiologisms), or a particular personal characteristic (idiopathy). Each story is an idiomorphous particle of one's sense-of-self. Idiosyncratic to one's "self" is the sum total of his experiences in story form. Each interpretation is distinctly different from anyone else's interpretation, and each time one self-narrates, *that* characterization is idiomatic.

Perhaps Carl von Sydow simply wanted us to realize that there is a difference between stories that we tell which involve our own experiences and those that do not, and he labeled them memorates to designate that which is purely a personal narrative of one's own experiences (1934). It is not a difficult concept to uphold—that we do indeed have experiences which cannot be duplicated by anyone else, and the interpretation is one's own and unique. One's personal experience as later told by another is quite different in emotion and wording and is always subject to change, especially after further tellings.

Yet another dimension is added to the study of narrating: that process which takes place within the individual *before* one narrates to another, and that process is both similar to and different from narrating between individuals. This affects all of us, for all individuals' cognitive processes mark what is distinctive to *homo sapiens* and *homo narrans*. The basic stories which we tell to ourselves are possible antecedents for action; we may consciously be formulating a plan by depicting a situation in which we visualize specific activity, or unconsciously verbalizing situations which seem to be in need of action. The communitas which is desired by all as the ultimate understanding may be only within "self." Domestic abuse and homeless victims may know how to solve the societal problems which plague our nation, but the solutions may still be in the idionarrating stage, as told by and to selves. Those selves may not be able to enter "normal" discourse with others, for what impresses us is the *kind* of individual whom we conceptualize as "innovator." The bag lady who spends her days meandering in what seems to be a world of her own is not viewed by well-dressed and working community members as capable of articulating legitimate personal, social, and political concerns—and positing solutions. Her persona is "tarnished." What possible value, people ask, would there be in listening to *her* narrating?

The next chapter will address the topic of personal experience narratives by victims (as told to others), with analysis of their expressiveness in regard to societal issues.

CHAPTER THREE

Victims' Narratives: Expression of Personal, Social, and Political Concerns

Mary Alice Donovan, age 66, of Palms, California, often expresses her feelings in poetry (1986):

The screams weren't mine,
She said in haste
(A bruise was hidden at her waist).

His first wife didn't understand him,
She said in tears.
(Why was her child consumed by fear?)

I didn't mean to shoot the gun,
She said in court.
(The jury knew 'twas last resort).

Home is just a fantasy,
She said, alone
(and sucking on a meatless bone).

He lives just fine, with all that's mine,
She said of her abuser.
(Who couldn't wait to lose her).

And now he has another wife,
She said beside her cart
(Which once belonged to Safeway's mart).

The screams won't be *mine*,
She says in haste.
There won't be bruises at *my* waist.

I'll change his ways, you'll see,
For he insists he doth love *me*.

Unlucky is the number three. . . .

Mary Alice is not a poet who is likely to be widely read, for she spends her days wandering, talking aloud to herself, and gesturing to all. Mary Alice is a bag lady, and most people judge her by sight as a "crazy person" and assume that she lacks the ability to perceive or articulate rationally any personal and/or societal problems. Since "we" assume that "normal" people may occasionally talk to themselves in private (but not in public) and their body language is part of that "normal" narrating process, it follows that what (mentally-ill drifter) Mary Alice performs in public must necessarily be verbal garbage.

Her personal story as told in poetry is not rambling nonsense; it is her reconstruction of a noteworthy happening which embodies a distinct message with social and political overtones: she was a battered wife with a home, was acquitted of shooting her abuser, and she is now homeless while he lives comfortably with another wife whom Mary Alice knows will also be beaten. One has to wonder why Mary Alice did not have an attorney to represent her interests. If one has the patience to listen to her personal narratives, Mary Alice will explain, and her experiences are quite similar to Janie's (age 61, Los Angeles, California, 1987):

> He used me, you see. I had money, and he bought everything he wanted. And then he married me so that it was all legal; he could have it all if only he could get rid of me. He beat me silly. He threatened our son by breaking his toys if he didn't obey the strictest of commands. I called the police, but when they came, Rodney said I was crazy and he wanted me committed. He said I abused our son, and he wanted custody. After five years of pain and humiliation, I took his gun and shot him in the leg as he came at me intending to punch me in the stomach. I went to jail. He got our son. No one believed me, because he was so popular in our town, and I was just a dumb housewife who didn't even mix in. I couldn't, you see, because he wouldn't let me have any friends; I was a prisoner in our house. So when I got out of jail, I found

that he had filed for divorce, and no lawyer was interested in helping me, so I started for California where I had a sister. But she died of cancer just before I finally got here, and I just sort of began living in one neighborhood behind stores where I could find a shed or bin, and dumped food and clothing. They built this mall last year, and now I live much better. I can sit here most of the day. I sure do wish some lawyer would have helped me. I bought the house he still lives in with his newest wife. *Something* ought to be mine. . . .

While the battered and homeless are in danger of being scrutinized only as "groups," the folklorist possesses the skills to elicit personal experience narratives for evidence as to the different ways in which individuals (and women in particular) have become and remain victims of abuse and homelessness. Even though the stories may often be performed in a crude or refined manner, may be clever or pedestrian, prudent or brash, and told in verbal and non-verbal modes, the language of victimization and/or poverty can be a compelling commentary on contemporary society. Dell Hymes speaks to the role of folklore (1975: 350):

> The concern of folklore with specific means, on the one hand, and with identity and values, on the other, enables it, if it will, to bridge the gap that has frustrated efforts to understand language and communication so long. . . . Language has . . . not been seen as something embedded and meaningful in human life, for lack of a perspective which folklore can help bring.

What is aesthetically performed by people in crisis pertains to personal, social, and political concerns. Most often these categories overlap. The concept, language, and symbolism of warfare is such an exemplification, and is expressed by Sandi (age 27, Los Angeles, California, 1986):

> For years I was a prisoner of war. Maybe that's not really right, because I could have left. But I married right after high school and had kids. Tom made me give up my friends because he didn't like them. What he didn't like was that I might have a life of my own. Anyway, I was like a prisoner in our little house. I didn't have a car, and he

never gave me money for a bus or anything else. Our social life was strictly church on Sunday and he never let me out of his sight. We watched TV every night, and all he'd allow were violent things, like war movies, and cop shows, or the fights. Everything was someone killing or maiming. When he went off to work I got to see what life was like for other people. Not that I think everyone lives like the soaps, but all kinds of ways of living come up. And I got to see the news. He never cared what was happening outside of his job. He never voted, so I didn't get to vote. He'd take the oldest kids to school, he did the shopping, and he took the kids to the doctor. I can't ever remember getting out and doing anything for myself, or having any fun at all. I was so dependent on him that I hated him and wished he would die. But then, what if he *did* die? I couldn't get along by myself after so many years. So I was terrified that he might die. He'd hit me for asking to go "out." He'd hit me for doing something he didn't like "in." So I loved and hated him, letting him torture me and waiting for it just to know that I was still, well, important, I guess. If he ignored me it was worse than being hurt by him. My house was a prison compound, and Tom was my captor, and I needed attention of any kind from the cruel captor. I saw a story on TV with a woman like that. I escaped by calling a hotline. I guess I'm free. But here I am in a *shelter*. The doors are locked, bars on the windows, and someone always telling me what to do. How will I ever get the chance to live like I want to? I got no chance.

Children are also affected, as Ricky (age 26, of Long Beach, California, 1985) notes:

When Phil put bars on our windows I thought, gee, now it really looks like a prison, too. Before it was all in my mind. He was the 'Nam guard and I was the prisoner. I was a POW in America. I know how the men must have felt, being in a prison camp. Can't get away, being tortured, and being completely in your guard's hands. I know it sounds nutty, but at first it was a kind of kinky sex thing; it didn't frighten me as much as it should have. Then he got more violent, and it wasn't like playing at being a "captive woman." He controlled me. He'd come home early so he could tie me up and use me until he was tired. I waited for him to do just that. But I wasn't enjoying it like he was. I was the one being hurt and then being ignored. But I needed the attention he was giving me, and I didn't have any from anyone else. I don't have any friends out here, and my whole life was with Phil. He was my lover, if you can call what he does loving, but more than that he was my warden, keeping me from doing anything I wanted. I think we leeched off of each other's needs. When Phil said the bars were for our protection, I felt funny. I couldn't get *out*, either. The kids think bars are fun because they can play their war games better with bars. That's all they do play, because Phil only lets them buy war toys. So now my kids play war games and prisoners and guards. That's real life, though, isn't it? War is everywhere. How do I change our lives? My alternative is going to the streets. We won't be safe there. It's only the survival of the fittest in another war.

The prisoner of war theme and syndrome is a very common one among abused women in domestic settings. Sandi and Ricky recognize the symbiotic relationship that develops between the victim and the victimizer. Studies of prisoners of war and hostages of terrorists delineate the ways in which the abused come to depend on the attention of their abusers, just as the abusers depend on their victims for immediate and continuing satisfaction. A particular relationship develops between the one who hurts and the one who is being hurt, and I believe that the operative word is "dependence." The mutual "need" or dependence is not one of compatibility, but one which is born in physical and/or psychological intimacy and grows with time and is intensified in relative isolation. A definite and vital motif or theme is needed for this type of interaction: a wartime hostage situation, a philosophical terrorist activity, or a domestic hostage scenario creates a situation which fosters mutual dependence. There is no "attachment" formed between store clerk and customer which results in the emotional base necessary for binary opposites: love/hate, torture/relief, need/disregard, attention/deprivation, or pleasure/pain. There is a tendency for binary opposites to merge psychologically within lengthy and intimate conditions; dependence based in constant feedback and response blurs reality and causes a perceptual distortion of personae. The need for each other and the anticipation of each person fulfilling an expected role to continue existence under specified circumstances creates a mutual understanding of such roles, thereby encouraging the acceptance of role-playing to the point that the individuals lose their grip on reality and begin to exist in a surrealistic realm. Perhaps there is an empathy for the other which transcends the personal experience; in psychoanalytic terms, symbiosis results when introjection (an unconscious psychic process which transfers representative images) occurs. From the many stories I have heard, I hypothesize that one very important reason why women stay with men who "put them through hell" is due to this symbiotic and parasitic relationship which is only comprehensible when seen as analogous to a captor and his captive.

It is interesting to note that I proposed this hypothesis in the early 1980s while acting as house support staff at a shelter for battered women, and discussed it often with prosecutors and public defenders while victim advocate for the city attorney's office. Virtually no one respected my thoughts on the topic. I pursued this concept/syndrome in conference papers, but because they were never submitted for publication, my first written documentation appeared in my dissertation (completed in 1988) and not one word has been changed in this "revision." A major article appeared in the *Los Angeles Times* in 1991 (August 20, E1): "The baffling problem of why abused women often remain in harmful relationships is undergoing a radical, new appraisal by mental health experts. They now say these women exhibit a behavior that can develop in classic hostage situations." The long article continues to describe exactly what I have been trying to get practitioners to consider. The study was presented by University of Cincinnati psychologist Edna Rawlings at the annual meeting of the American Psychological Association, (August 1991), and the recognition of this syndrome is to "understand how therapists are able to develop more effective techniques to help women free themselves." Many scholars find themselves in this position; we are not always the first to be acknowledged as noting a particular concept. What I find intriguing is that until a *psychologist* brought this very common sense syndrome to other psychologists' attention, somehow it was not "legitimate." As a folklorist (not the best "name/label" for a respectable scholarly discipline!) and (volunteer community member) service provider, my understanding and verbal delineation of an extremely important hypothesis was ignored. That would seem to negate my proposal that academics should be activists in community and societal affairs. But that is not so, for 1) I know that my dissertation was read by other scholars and some of the material has been quoted in others' academic works, and 2) I am correct: a scholar, whether it be folklorist or psychologist, *has* become the catalyst for meaningful new thought, mental health therapy, and social change.

This distinctive hostage (captor/captive) relationship has unusual ramifications for the victims, and I suggest that the trained folklorist is best prepared to analyze one particular circumstance for its significance in understanding the human condition. During the long period in which I have been listening to the stories of women physically and emotionally abused by husbands or lovers, I have heard a disproportionate number of tales of supranormal experiences. Specifically, I refer to a phenomenon which has been the subject of study as "nightmare" and the "Old Hag." Henry Fuseli's (1781) painting "The Nightmare" (followed by a 1782 version) represents the traditional experience: a terrifying bedroom intruder hovering over a flaccid and recumbent figure. This apparently universal phenomenon has been labeled, for example, "the Mare" in 16th century England, *Mara* in Sweden, *augumangia* and *ukomiarik* among the Eskimo/Inuit, and "the Old Hag" in Newfoundland and America. The original term "Nightmare" comes from the Anglo-Saxon *neaht* or *nicht* and *mara*: night incubus/succubus, and became intermingled with the use of "hag" (from the Old English term *haegtesse* [harpy or witch]) in English folklore, where hags and witches were correlated (Simpson 1973: 72, 87). As English culture crossed the Atlantic Ocean, it became ensconced in Newfoundland where the tradition of being attacked in the night by a witch or hag became part of being "hagrid" (possibly from hagged and/or haggard and/or hag-ride), and the term the "Old Hag" is still in use to describe a person who has been victimized at night by a witch (Hufford 1982). In the United States, the word "nightmare" is used to describe bad dreams and is still recognized as reference to the tradition of a "hag" attacking a sleeping individual. The forthcoming *Encyclopedia of American Popular Beliefs and Superstitions* (from the archive collection founded by Wayland D. Hand at the University of California, Los Angeles) will include references of local beliefs about the "Old Hag" as well as witch-riding (a correlated experience in which the victim is saddled, bridled, and ridden by a witch).

While none of the informants expressed any knowledge of the traditional phenomenon, the experiential features of the syndrome remain the same: 1) the event is perceived by the victim as occurring while awake, not asleep; 2) there is the impression of a figure near one's bed (or place of repose), sometimes accompanied by auditory and olfactory stimuli, and often in conjunction with a light behind or around the figure; 3) in some manner the victim is completely unable to move during the experience; 4) the victim feels oppressed—by pressure on the chest or a choking sensation—which inhibits breathing; 5) the setting in which the experience takes place is described accurately in terms of the victim's actual location, in contrast to an imaginary setting; 6) fear is expressed—of the attacker, the experience itself, impending death, or the unknown.

David Hufford's extensive study of "hagging" and its implications in the area of sleep research has provided many insights, especially in terms of the phenomenon being experience-centered as opposed to culture-bound (1982). His research was conducted in a manner different from mine, and our findings have some significant variances. Hufford's investigation was based on structured interviews of people who experienced such attacks whom he located by speaking publicly about the syndrome, and follow-up interviews in which he participated as an interviewer. I, on the other hand, listened avidly to victims' accountings of "bad nights," "weird afternoon naps," "crazy experiences," and "reasons for finally leaving abusers." I did not interrupt the narratives with questions, as did Hufford, and I gave no indication of knowing a traditional phenomenon to which the teller might relate and thereby be influenced. By this means I garnered "hagging" experiences within narratives which were in progress as natural expressions of victims' distress. This is important because I as researcher encouraged an atmosphere of open-ended narrating in which I provided no suggestive or prejudicial commentary. Whatever victims expressed concerning their plight was of importance, and because of the unusual data base I have formulated hypotheses which vary from Hufford's.

One hypothesis which I propose pertains to the sexual connotation of the "Old Hag" assault. Hufford is adamant that there is no connection between a true hagging experience and sexuality (1982: 131):

> The presence of overt sexual content as a frequent feature of the nightmare proper is highly debatable. I have encountered a few explicit sexual details in Old Hag accounts, but these are rare and are not typically major components of a given experience. Some overtly sexual accounts have appeared in the course of my investigation, but these differed from the Old Hag in that they have lacked the paralysis feature and, in several cases, fear. These probably constitute either a distinct subtype of the experience or a different phenomenon altogether. . . . It would be a mistake automatically to assume that no more realistic experience lies behind the widespread incubus traditions. To do so would invite a repetition of the errors and confusion that have characterized writings about the Old Hag variety of experience.

Donald Ward, on the other hand, remarks in "The Return of the Dead Lover: Psychic Unity and Polygenesis Revisited" (1980: 313):

> I have noted that, although the subject frequently denies anything sexual in the encounter, their descriptions tell us otherwise. . . . . When a woman is lying on her back in bed, and a good-looking man (real or imagined) is stroking her legs, there is surely something sexual in the experience, whether she perceives it as such or not. . . . In many of the cases, the subjects deny a sexual component (even though it is obviously present). In other cases the subjects perceive the encounter as intensely sexual.

From the narratives of my informants I must consider that there is indeed a relationship between sexual intimacy and the "Old Hag" apparitional attack. This may be due to a direct correlation between the real life situations of the victims of violence and the "hallucinatory" experiences. The "hagging" experienced by Adriana (age 23, Los Angeles, California, 1986) exemplifies many which are rife with sexual symbolism:

> Well, I make up my mind not to go back with my husband. I not to take any pain anymore. I tell you again about why, but I feel some strange about talking into your machine, so maybe I not tell it the same, and you'll tell me if I do not. I not ever forget what happened. But I look at the machine and know I not talking to you like before! I say I decide not to see him again. I feel that God has told me. No, not to tell me but to give me a sign maybe. Last month I am in the hospital again and the social worker is trying to get me to call the shelter because Raoul has beaten me too much, and this time cut me with his switchblade. I don't want to leave him, since I am illegal and will be deported if I have no Raoul. So I go back and I tell him that if he does not go to counseling, I am to leave. He promises never to touch me again, and for maybe a week he is nice and not hurt me in bed, and then he gets drunk and cuts me again. I let my friend take me to the police, and I sign the paper. He calls me at my friend's and swears that he is going to AA and to counseling, and maybe I'll not go to court. I say okay, because I just find out I'm pregnant, and the baby must have the father. I lie in bed at my friend's, and I'm thinking about this baby, and thinking that maybe it shouldn't be with a man like Raoul. Then God gives me a sign. He makes Raoul come flying like a black cloud into the window, which I can see is full of sun. Raoul is changing shape, like the clouds full of rain, and he is growing. Larger than before he is growing, and as he changes the shape he is getting bigger until the big black cloud is over me, rumbling like the thunder. Then the rain falls on me, but is Raoul lying on me, and he is *so* heavy that I no can breathe. I am dying from not getting breath. I see his big switchblade moving in the cloud. It is Raoul and the cloud all in one. The blade is coming at me and I no can move. I try to call for my friend, and no sound comes out for I no can breathe. God must then tell Raoul to leave me alone for I then can breathe and the cloud is going out the window. But I see it is now smoke from the burning trash outside, and I know

that I must get up and close the window. But I am so weak from being afraid that I can barely move, and for all day I pray. I know that I not to have this baby with Raoul. I go back to mother and sisters in Argentina. Safer.

While sexual *symbolism* is typified in Adriana's story, Amy (age 37, Lancaster, Pennsylvania, 1978) expresses a more explicit experience, another in which the victim experiences paralysis during the attack:

> I just lay down on the sofa to catch a relief from the kids. It was drizzling out, but I had the window open, and I was staring at the drops dripping down the sill onto the wallpaper. I was thinking about closing the window when the sun suddenly filled the sky and Frank was walking right in through the window. I know that sounds crazy, but this great big man just came in, which is kind of funny anyway since Frank is a little guy, and he stood on the edge of the sofa. He towered over me and leered at me just the way he always did when he wanted sex. I knew if I didn't give him exactly what he wanted, I'd get my face punched, so I just lay there watching him. I mean, I couldn't have moved if I'd wanted to because I felt almost paralyzed. He threw himself on me and crushed me into the sofa. I could feel him pushing down too hard and his bullets belt buckle was jabbing me. He kept pushing up and down on me like I was being stabbed with the belt buckle each time. I felt like all the air was being pushed out of my lungs and I tried to pull away but couldn't move at all. I was so tired that I just gave up and began to cry. But I wasn't crying. I wasn't moving at all or breathing for a minute, and then he drifted off me like a leaf and blew right out the window, getting smaller and smaller until I was looking at a raindrop dripping down from the wallpaper. It was the most scary thing that ever happened to me, and I can't understand any of it. I don't think I was asleep. I was wide awake. I know one thing for sure. I am cured of Frank forever.

The use of a weapon by the "hagging" abuser has both realistic and symbolic significance. Statistics by the U.S. Department of Justice reveal that in 21% of violent victimizations by an intimate, the offender used or showed a weapon. . .equally as likely to be guns, knives, and other objects used as weapons

(Harlow 1991: 6). The weapon almost always described by the abused has been of phallic shape: knife, gun, broom handle, baseball bat, or hammer. Further, it is usually "jabbed" or "thrust" (often repeatedly) into the woman's abdominal or chest region, rendering her breathless or exhausted. The actual experiences of abuse by husband or lover have involved those same weapons. The fear expressed has been carried over from real life to supranormal experience, especially in relation to type of assault; beatings are frequently associated with pre- or post-intercourse, and women often are beaten for the first time during pregnancy. While staff at shelters for battered women, the police, service providers, and prosecutors/public defenders are aware of abuse during pregnancy, a study reported by the Surgeon General's Office cited that 25% of all obstetrical patients are abused women, an even higher percentage than in the emergency service (1985: 20).

Another feature which is often mentioned by victims is the larger-than-life size of the attacker. While it might not seem peculiar that an apparition would appear larger than an ordinary person, the women have been impressed by the disparate size between the husband and the "hagging" figure. This makes sense when one considers the undue amount of control that an abuser employs in many a (physically or psychologically) battered woman's life and in the supranormal experience. The smaller/real-life man exercised physical and emotional control over his wife, but she had always managed to manipulate the situation by being able to *move*. None of the victims of the supranormal assault could move, indicating a *greater* degree of vulnerability and possible death. Fear preceded the attack, fear was ever-present in the victim's mind, and fear was magnified during the apparitional appearance. Richard Gelles notes that women are faced with a no-win situation. It seems to make no difference whether or not the abused woman fights back. Her failure to be aggressive leaves her passively at the abuser's mercy, and conversely, if she does aggressively protect herself, she is likely to be more viciously beaten (Gillespie 1989: 132). This no-win situation only reinforces the perception of the abuser as larger-than-life when in this particularly unusual situation.

The time of the "hagging" experience has, in past research, been assumed if not noted as "at bedtime," or "at night just before sleep." There are three time facets in our lives: awake, asleep, and the period just before or after sleep. The latter is considered to put one into an "altered" state of consciousness which is neither strictly awake or asleep. The period just before sleep is called the hypnagogic state, and the period just before waking is the hypnopompic state. In perhaps half of the cases I have documented the victim experienced a "hagging" during the daytime hours, most commonly while watching television, reading, or resting. This would suggest that the women—usually self-described as lethargic, tired, or depressed—became mesmerized while staring at something, and the episode occurred during the hypnagogic state. In Helen Neuborne's testimony at the Biden hearings in 1990, she refers to statistics reported by Straus and Gelles in *Physical Violence in American Families: Risk Factors and Adaptations to Violence in 8145 Families* (1990: 426). Relevant to the "hagging" experiences, results of the studies include abused women revealing that they spent twice as many days in bed as other women; having twice as many headaches; and suffering four times the rate of depression. And according to Roberta Thyfault's study, battered women develop skills of survival rather than escape. They focus on what is occurring immediately, on what they need to do to make it through the day, basing their evaluation of what method of coping will subject them to the least amount of danger (1984: 490). All of these references and the material I garnered from personal narratives lead us to understand that abused women have a tendency to be more susceptible to fatigue and daytime resting than non-abused women. The woman who saw her husband becoming smaller as he disappeared from view was probably in the hypnopompic state which has been associated with the awakening process, the gradual disappearance of the apparition reflecting the gradual return to full consciousness. Maria (age 22, La Habra, California, 1984) implies that a (daytime) contemplation of an encounter with a batterer (at dinnertime) is "exhausting":

> I made lasagna fifteen times in a row last month for Eddie. He said it was the only thing I made that he liked,

but I think he just does that to annoy me. He knows it is hard for me to make those homemade noodles with this broken arm. So one day last month I just left the noodles boiling and sat down for a few minutes. I felt like I couldn't stand up if an earthquake hit. I hated suppers. He'd come home either drunk or angry or ready to find something wrong and I'd have to eat with my heart in my mouth waiting for something to happen. Anyway, I was just sort of sprawled on the couch when I saw the front door open and in he came. In the afternoon. I tried to get up and couldn't. His face was all screwed-up with anger that I was on the couch, and he came at me and jumped on top of me and tried to smother me. I tried to yell but nothing came out. I was terrified and knew that this time he would kill me for sure. I got my breath back just as the telephone was ringing. I remember thinking that he left because the phone rang and his boss was looking for him. I felt awful, but I got up quick and fixed those noodles proper. I didn't need another broken arm. You know, I left the next day.

The breaking of a behavioral norm set by society has been cited by Lauri Honko (1962) as an occasion for a supranormal encounter; I would consider that in many cases in which the wife lives under particular conditions set by her husband (the establishment and belief in a set behavioral norm), the same type of experience might be triggered by the breaking of the "house rule." Instead of perceiving a culturally meaningful figure during the time of distress, the battered wife's brain might be filling in the image of the person she fears will discover her improper behavior, thus providing *Gestalterganzung* (the completion of the form). In other words, by fearing Frank, Amy stared at the raindrops on her wallpaper and in a psychophysical state of exhaustion and stress, her brain filled in the image of Frank in front of her. This application of perception psychology (espoused by Nilsson/Eskerod [1936, 1947] and Honko [1962], as modifications of von Sydow's hypothesis [1929]) illuminates the dominating concerns of the abused woman: her survival depends on her subjugation and ability to please her partner. Everything she perceives is within the scope of this internal dominating concern, while any deviation from the expected behavioral pattern would be an external concern. In most of the cases the women were relatively deprived of sensory stimuli; they were alone and either without "noise" or that "noise" was of such nature as to be mesmerizing—perhaps in the sensory overload sense. A lack of external stimulation probably contributed to the mind and eye being deceived by the internal stimulation of personal concerns.

Rudolf Otto has termed the strong reaction of fear, fascination, awe, and reverence as "numinous" (1953). Eve (age 28, Los Angeles, California, 1986) expresses such feelings of numinosity which are typical of those which are part of the "visitations":

> I had to spend two months in the locked ward last year. I had this awful dream twice in a row, and I told the doctor that it wasn't no dream, but he put me away anyway. I know that Harvey came into my room in the hospital and tried to kill me, but the doctor said he was in jail at the time. I *know* that I was sort of drowsy on medication from surgery, but I was awake enough to be watching a TV show and I could tell the doctor what it was about. He says I was nuts because I said that Harvey came at me with his big old knife and lay down on me in the bed and put the knife right up to my throat and pressed the handle so tight against my vocal cords that I couldn't scream for help. I lay there and sweated and choked and looked into his eyes. He was all blurry, and I guess that was my medication, but he was there and I felt every hair on my body being touched. When I told the nurse, she told the doctor, and he said I was crazy and they put me away. I know what happened, and it scares me even today. If that hadn't happened, though, I probably would be dead, but I never went back. I been on my own ever since, and as scared as I am now being alone all the time and not knowing where I'll sleep tomorrow, I was more scared then.

It is not unusual for the person who describes a supranormal experience to be thought of and labeled as mentally ill. Stark and Flitcraft (1988: 303) note that "battered women are far more likely than non-battered women to be given a pseudopsychiatric label such as hysteric, hypochondriac, crock, etc." It is undoubtedly a major factor in the dearth of such taletellings.

Victims of domestic abuse have an added burden: few people believe that any woman in her right mind would stay with a man who beats her. Consequently, the victim keeps "secret" many of the stories which she would like to share with others. Ward (1980: 313) concludes that

> this numinous component ultimately contributes to a process of mental therapy. . . . Time and time again I have noted that the feeling of numinosity which accompanies the encounter is so intense that the subject is shocked into looking directly at previously suppressed problems, and into taking action to resolve those problems.

I have discovered in my research that when the frightening experience of the supranormal encounter is greater than the actual abuse by her husband, it is not unusual for the wife to decide that she has to leave the violent situation. It may not be until much later that she can articulate this decision to others; it seems to be a gut feeling at the time of the experience and is acted upon without explanation to others. This is understandable in light of the attitude which others would form. Ward has also raised questions concerning these extraordinary experiences and possible predilections thereto. Particular individuals, posits Ward, are predisposed to numinous experiences: the creative, the emotionally shattered, those who believe in witches and/or ghosts, the religious, and those who are repressing problems (1977). My research points to yet another population: victims of violence (usually physical, but psychological abuse as well). Many of the women, of course, are repressing the problems attendant to the necessity of leaving their homes and current lifestyle.

In summary, then, the major characteristics of the hagging experience as related by victims of violence are those of the traditional encounter and the "ugliness" or distorted features of the "hagger," the symbolic or explicit sexual connotation, an attack by the person who has abused her in actual interaction, the use of a weapon which has been used by the abuser, and at a time element which is related to the victim's exhaustion (or stress, or illness). After effects which may be traced to the hagging experience have been identified by victims as headaches (perhaps migraine), ulcers, rashes, mouth sores, disgust regarding sexual activities, and a plan to escape from the abuser.

The recognition of the attacker as the person she fears most in her everyday life (who uses the same form of assault) is a particularly important feature. It is obvious that a known attacker, especially one with whom she has had an intimate relationship and by whom she has been "betrayed," would have an extremely impressionable impact on the victim. That husband (or lover) has been a stakeholder in the victim's life. If they have children, all are stakeholders in "the family." These are factors which can be easily understood by the victim. What is not so obvious but just as intriguing is Ian Mitroff's concept of "internal stakeholders of the psyche" (1983: 86-87):

> Every aspect of a person's existence is capable of being turned into an archetypal symbol, image, or character. . . . An archetype, or image that represents it. . . contains the essence of a particular human experience that has been repeated enough to make a permanent but not necessarily unattenable print on neutral structure. . . . [They] include such prototypical experiences as. . . father, mother, authority, self, femininity. . . devil . . . maleness and sleep. If we look at the core or essence of a symbol, according to the laws pertaining to subjective processes, we will find evidence for archetypal influences.

Consequently, Mitroff postulates that "each archetype is an idealized image, more pure and extreme, and larger than life, to help us cope with and understand the complexities of life" (1983: 88). An archetype, then, may reveal itself as a harpy or hag or any significant traditional form, or as a grotesque and amorphous shape, or as the actual image of an abuser; this figure represents the stakeholder in the victim's life, buried within the deep layers of the mind as a "devil/evil" influence and able to appear and reappear, larger than life, to perform some coping task. That event may occur in the hypnagogic state as well as in dreams—which are basically recognized as the time for experiencing archetypal imagery. "Such [archetypic] beings represent an individual's terrifying internal nature concretized and projected out onto external reality in an attempt to cope with his or her inner and outer fears" (1983: 86).

Personal concerns become societal concerns when individual problems affect others and the ways in which we live, learn, work, pray, and play together, i.e., in our interactions within our communities. The effects of domestic abuse rarely affect just one person—the victim. If children are not involved (with psychological and/or physical deterioration), parents, friends, neighbors, religious leaders, service providers, and legal systems almost always are. The abuser's effect eventually leads to mandatory interaction with the court system, counseling groups, or community services.

Children of victimization are affected in various ways. It has been noted in numerous studies and television "specials" (none of which I intend to cite or question) that male children tend to become abusers in later life, and that female children tend to lend themselves to abusive relationships as wives/partners. We see teen runaways and prostitutes of both sexes on our streets. Hypothetically many of these are children who have been victimized at home and are either forced to leave or choose what they assume will be a "better life" elsewhere. I have been in the company of abused and/or homeless women with either too aggressive or extremely passive children in tow. I can only assume that each child develops according to a combination of genetics and environment, but I have every reason to believe that environment makes the stronger mark. Marie (age 35, Santa Monica, California, 1987) explains what happens in her home:

> I want to drop the charges against my husband. If I had known that by calling the police he would end up being arrested and booked, I think I would rather take more beatings. He was back at the house before the children and I, who followed him to the police station. He was so angry that while he didn't hit me right away because he knows that until he goes to court to plead not guilty, he has to be good, he will never forget or forgive me. We will always have a strained relationship, and it will never be one of love again. The children are afraid of him now, because they feel his anger. They still fight all of the time, but when he is around, they are very quiet. Maybe they think they will set him off, like a time bomb. Maybe that is the wrong word, for he is always ready to explode; there is

not a time when he apologizes or pretends that he is sorry
for his behavior. We have had a stormy time of it, with no
relief. There has always been a lot of yelling in the house.
The [four] children mimic their father's behavior,
screaming at each other and hitting whenever something
doesn't suit them. Even though they are all girls, they act
just as he does in any situation. I see it getting worse every
year. But my only alternative is to give up everything we
own. What will happen then? The girls will blame me for
having nothing, and that will not make them happier. I am
trapped.

Abused women are so often told by ministers, elders,
priests, rabbis and other religious leaders that it is their religious
duty to stay with their husbands no matter how bad the situation
that one wonders about the "cost" of religiosity. I have yet to
hear of a religious leader telling a wife to leave her husband. The
church, perhaps more than any other institution, is responsible
for forcing the *woman* to "keep the family together." *She* can go
to counseling if she likes, but the duty appears to be hers alone.
While there are some marital counseling groups related to
churches, there are none that I know of dealing with the
counseling of batterers alone. The worst example I have heard
relating to a wife's "duty" to "be under her husband" is one I
have on videotape (1987) by Dr. Gene Scott, one of television's
most popular evangelists (although he sneers at the appellation,
preferring to be called a "teacher"). In all fairness, at times he
does refer to women "leaving jerks," but that is not his stand on
what the Bible teaches: man owing allegiance to God and women
owing allegiance to man. Since he has (also on videotape)
screamed, "I hate her!" (referring to his ex-wife) I fear his
parishioners are confused about their "duty" to man and marriage. Rachel (age 23, Los Angeles, California, 1987) expresses
such distress:

You know that Doc says we are superior to men, but he
insists that the Bible says we aren't and must be
subservient to men. I have been a member of the Westcott
Faith Center for years, and I really respect Doc's
intelligence. I asked for marital counseling, and was told
that he wouldn't do that because each of us has to make
our own decision. I was told that sinners were welcome in

church. But it was made perfectly clear that I was to look up what I was to do in the Bible, and I was given Chapter and Verse. So I guess I have to stay. But Doc is divorced. I don't know what to do. I certainly don't want to go to Hell because I didn't interpret the Bible right. If I call the police the next time Bob hits me am I committing a sin?

Abusive behavior by husbands may lead to family disintegration and the formation of yet another family with the same problems. The nuclear family is increasingly being replaced by binuclear families: post-divorce households in which more relationships and intimate problems are created. In studies such as Grossman's (1985: 5), battered women report that they do not perceive shelters as viable options since it means leaving one's family unit and home. This value on the family and marriage and wanting to keep things intact outweigh violence. Bettina (age 43, York, Pennsylvania, 1975) expresses a typical problem:

We have so many children between us that I can't keep count anymore. But it only means that all of our problems got multiplied. Tim beats or threatens all of us, and the doctors just try to palm us off on someone else. We're a real pain. [She laughed and winced at the same time. It was not meant to be a "funny" comment.] I don't know what to do now, and neither do the other two wives. We can't keep all of the kids away from him, and there will always be another next wife. . . .

The study of family interactions has been of interest to family folklorists. With the recognition by Mody Boatright of the family "saga" (to denote that lore which focuses on the family group, which the members believe to be the truth, and is perpetuated by oral transmission [1958]), questions were raised pertaining to the forms and motifs of stories which revolve around the family. When Stanley Brandes analyzed "family misfortune stories" (1975), he noted not only the recurring tale type but also a type of tale which acts as a form of apology or explanation for family failures or weaknesses. Family folklore may tell scholars, social service providers, therapists, and the general public more about domestic life than has been realized. Aside from the value of gaining insights into cultural beliefs,

values, and customs, the stories and jokes which family members
tell about relatives and experiences provide information which is
not usually shared with people outside of the family. It is not
likely, for example, that stories would be told to strangers about
Grandpa beating Grandma, or Uncle Bill seducing his daughter.
But within the family these stories are known and passed along,
and the folklorist pursuing family tales of victimization is apt to
evoke such hidden dramas of domestic life. The family "saying"
(e.g., "Only one wife to give!") may be a few words understood
by everyone in the family as representative of a story which has
particular significance. The Fragan family's use of that phrase
refers to an incidence of domestic abuse which has been ignored
in its victimization sense by the males and taken seriously by the
females, who often use it as a "warning" or moral for other
women in the family. I was an invited guest at an extended-
family dinner (in Los Angeles in 1983) when Mrs. Fragan burned
her hand on a pan, screamed in pain, and Mr. Fragan laughingly
waved his arm as he said, "I'm sorry that I only have one wife to
give for my country!" Later that evening, Mrs. Fragan told me
this story, which is known and told by all in the family; it is
considered to be a tradition.

> Uncle Sascha was an artist. He was too cheap to hire
> models, so he used his wife—and she hated posing.
> Especially since he painted only nudes, and he was also
> too cheap to put coins in the heater. This was Paris, you
> see, sometime around 1900. Anyway, she had constant
> colds, and even when she developed the flu, Sascha made
> her continue modeling. He, of course, wore a muffler and
> heavy clothing. One winter she died of pneumonia. He
> wasn't a nice man. But one of his paintings hangs in a
> French museum, so the family loves to claim him.

Mr. Fragan's version is slightly different:

> We have a very famous painter in our family—Sascha
> Perrault. His nude, Suzette, hangs in the Louvre. He was a
> frugal man who couldn't afford models, so his wife
> usually had to pose for him. One winter while he was
> trying to finish a painting, she upped and died on him.
> When he finally got a little deserved recognition, he

supposedly said, "I'm sorry that I had but one wife to give for my country."

The Pauley family has lived in central North Carolina for eight generations. They "recently lost their first kin to another state" (Mrs. Pauley's words) via the Fred Pauleys' move to California. Mrs. Pauley explained a family expression to me (in 1983), emphasizing the negative attitudes and behavior toward women in her family:

> I had me a cousin who did piece work. A real nothing job, but then he wasn't too much, anyway. Got fired from every nothing job he had before that. He'd get real ugly some nights. Usually after getting sotted. He'd beat up on poor Polly. You got to feel sorry for a woman stuck with the name Polly Pauley, anyway, don't you? So one night he came home particularly ugly, and pushed Polly around. He yelled, "I'll give you a piece of my mind." So nowadays we call him "piece work" whenever some man done something stupid.

Mr. Pauley heard her talking to me, and began to laugh. "You sure cleaned that up, Meg!" I asked what he meant, and she replied,

> Well, he's just got a dirty mind. That's the *point* of the story, you see. But old Fred here's talking about Polly saying, "You haven't got a piece to spare," and Jake giving it back, "Sure I do, you. And a smelly old piece you are, too." Fred's always talking dirty, especially when it comes to women's things. The *point* is that him who's stupid is 'piece work.' But that's Fred's way. He's not much one for saying anything good about women, and it's a poorly thing that he made sure our boys picked up on that, for they have more respect for a 'coon than their women.

The perception of women, wives, mothers, and stepmothers is reflected in the narrative motifs summarized in the *Motif-Index of Folk-Literature* (Thompson 1955-1958). If "woman" is "good" then she is almost always a victim. A man must take care of her, providing children with the notion that women cannot and should not be in control of their own lives. If "woman" is "bad," she is exemplified as shrew, overbearing, obstinate, nagging, disobedient, hag, lazy, stupid, unfaithful, deceptive, cruel, wicked, and offered as reward, sacrifice, or wager. Under "Wife," follows "see Adulteress." Under "Husband," however, follows "see Bridegroom." Under "Stepmother" there are twenty references to (cruel) women; under "Stepfather" there are but three references. These stories must at least subliminally affect attitudes and behavior; children especially would be influenced by such imagery.

Stith Thompson comments on wives (1946: 209):

> In folktales in general the wife is likely to be the object of pity and commiseration, so that some of the most beloved characters in the wonder tales are the long-suffering and persecuted heroines. But even in these same wonder tales cruelty often shows itself most merciless in faithless sisters, mothers, and wives. . . . In the folk anecdote, influenced perhaps by fabliaux and novelle with their medieval bias against women, the woman usually appears as wicked, overbearing, and faithless, or at best, unutterably stupid.

The importance of *family* in storytellings leads to a reevaluation of the significance of that phenomenon/institution as related to victimization and homelessness. Folklorists recognize that *homo sapiens* is, by his very nature, *homo religiosus, narrans, ludens,* and *faber.* I am hypothesizing that *homo sapiens* possesses a sense of familial association—a need to be psychologically (if not actively) linked with a personalized group which has blood or other bonding ties, and *homo sapiens* is therefore also *homo familias.* Evidence has not yet been presented of the universality among humankind as to man's *need* for familial relationships. I offer some evidence of such a need.

Families may consist of present, past, or wishful thinking relationships, by which I mean that one may be involved with an actual family—or fantasize about one desired. The most common form of fantasizing about "family" is the tracing of one's family tree, whereby one can root-up an ancestor or more who adds acclaim to one's self-image. (Mr. Fragan uses Uncle Sascha for this purpose.) However, fantasizing about one's ancestors—and characterizing those fantasies to others—is tantamount to grafting branches onto one's family tree: often individuals give attributes to ancestors which are not necessarily true, or completely fabricate an entire family. A fabricated family may be comprised of past or present associates, or be a figment of one's imagination. Members can be a symbolic representation of the family one could not have. A family may provide psychological satisfaction and reference for storytellings.

While my research focused on the female-homeless who have been victimized, I discovered a fascinating example of the need for family which I will impart: Mac the Hermit. Mac lives in the San Bernardino mountains of California near Big Bear Lake, in what he calls a cabin. In Beverly Hills it would be listed as a "rustic lodge." Externally and internally it is an exhibition of Mac's mastery of skills. An appreciation of nature is revealed in the variety of woods carved for practical and aesthetic purposes. The walls are adorned with intricate creations from forest debris; the furniture and the driftwood-mantle over the fireplace are formed from nearby "falls." Pictures of family are on tabletops, mantle, and walls. Mac says (1984):

> That's my Uncle Frederick. He won't be called Fred. He's a doctor in Phoenix. He's always trying to get me to move there, get a job, and live near my little nieces and nephews. They're all real smart. Now *this* picture is from Atlantic City. See the boardwalk chairs? My father used to peddle one. The one way up the boardwalk is him. My mother over here [he pointed] is riding a horse named Snowbird. We had wonderful summers in New Jersey and Pennsylvania. In this picture we're picnicking at the beach. Boy, were we ever rained out that day; a sudden storm. [Mac laughed and rubbed his arms.] The picture on the mantle is of my cousin Alan. He's with some movie star friends of his. He invited me to several of those Academy Award affairs, but I'm not really interested in those things. And that's my brother Andy. How I could tell you stories about his travels. He's been everywhere and he always wants me to go with him.

Mac likes to tell stories about his family. I heard about his parents, uncles, aunts, cousins, siblings, and assorted distant relatives. There is nothing unusual in that fact—except that Mac was orphaned at age two, never had any siblings, and as far as everyone knows, has no living relatives at all. Mac's "family album" is made up entirely of magazine pictures. I was flustered, and finally just remarked on the lovely picture frames. Our other companion mumbled something about "a nice, close family," and noted that with such fine-looking people it was strange that Mac chose to live as a hermit. Mac shrugged, and answered that he really didn't like cities—but *everyone* had a family, didn't they? I responded that many people are not particularly interested in relatives—and Mac looked astonished. "But we all *need* family," he answered.

This intense need for family (not related to religious or cultural tradition) may indeed be the major reason why women keep returning to the men who abuse them: the family tie may be a knot tighter and stronger than the "knot" caused by physical/emotional abuse. Further, the communitas which is developed and maintained—even through periods of discord—is so strong that "to be alone" is worse than traumatic happenings in a familial setting. To be able to say a few words to someone and have an entire past event recalled together is a rare experience. It does not seem to matter if that event was not a happy one; the family remains the quintessential support group, and communitas is remembered and desired. The sense of belonging appears to overcome or at least mask obstacles.

Family therapists have been thinking along similar lines. Family myths, which have been examined to some degree by folklorists, are also being studied by family therapists. Some believe that behavioral patterns may be defined by such strong beliefs. This was a topic of much interest at the 1985 (annual) meeting of the American Association for Marriage and Family Therapy. Dr. Dennis Bagarozzi analyzed the family myth in terms of the family member who is attributed with power as opposed to the member who actually determines what occurs. Discussion followed concerning the perpetuation of myths which are positive and useful to the family and those which are destructive to the family but serve functionally to provide immediate solutions to problems which the members do not wish to confront (1985). This is relevant to domestic violence and abuse because courts are now mandating counseling for (mainly first-offense) batterers, and it is doubtful if the topic of family myths arises in the course of the sessions. The shared beliefs in a particular *myth* may be directing behavior of family members away from the problems which they do not wish to acknowledge. It is extremely common for the batterer, victim, children, grandparents—and all relatives—to mask unacceptable behavior or to deny it altogether, albeit knowing that it exists. That distortion of reality which goes unchallenged may be an unconscious desire to keep the family together at all costs; but the family myth which "forecasts" that whatever happens in the family can be *"overcome"* is *not* useful or functional. It is destructive initially and intergenerationally. So the myth which for *some* families may be a positive force in familial "togetherness" may be for others only a way of covering up a problem of cyclic abuse. A diversion counselor could bring that myth to the forefront and use it as a therapeutic tool to assist the batterer— and through him other family members—to confront the masked issue.

In expressing themselves through storytelling, victims do seem to find a release, or relief, in the telling, for it is usually first with hesitation—and excuses—that women recount such experiences. Then, when the encounter has been told and no judgmental concern has been expressed by the listener, additional stories about victimization occur, either immediately or later, letting the trusted listener in on *more* intimate details of the victim's life. It is noteworthy that there has been an obvious reluctance among Asian and Native American women to divulge very personal problems in group settings. I attribute this to the nature of *our* multi-cultural grouping, in which the Asian or Native American was without cultural peers and possibly was overly self-conscious about "sharing." I believe that in a uni-cultural setting these women would have been more assertive in their participation in all aspects, and that is an area for further research. My feeling (which has been substantiated in informal discussion with Asian service providers) is that communitas among women bonded by *specific* cultural ties *plus* victimization of a similar nature evokes "sharing." One source indicated that within the large Pacific-Asian population there are such diverse cultural distinctions that "communitas" in the manner in which I expound would need to be reduced to specific cultural groups.

The intimate details of the lives of the abused and homeless are often inextricably tied to political issues. Amnesty and immigration are of current concern for many women. Their fears, while similar to those of alien males, must be different-iated. Carlotta (age 24, Los Angeles, California, 1987) expresses that which is indicative of the problems of many homeless women:

> If I report my husband to the law he will go to jail. What will happen to me and the children? While he is eating and sleeping in a warm place, we will be put on the street. I cannot apply for welfare. I cannot get a job because I tried and no one wanted me. We need the little money he brings in. If I get a divorce, I will not be allowed to apply for amnesty, because I have no job and no means of support. He won't help. He will just disappear like all the other men like him. They get in their trucks and move to another place. So I must let him do what he wants or I have to go back to Mexico. I have nothing there. We had no place to live. So what is better there?

Carolyn (age 33, Santa Monica, California, 1985) portrays a graphic picture of living conditions and comments on the politics of poverty:

> We been sleeping in missions for so long the kids don't know what a regular place is like, you know, like an apartment or a real house. I got kicked out of the coop we had. . . yeah, the place was an honest-to-God chicken coop. . . when the old man was sent up for stealing a car. . . . Once when we was in a really good mission—you know, with a lice-free bed—I read a newspaper. You know, the guys who run this country and give all that money to foreign countries are saying we here all got enough to eat and places to live so they voted to stop paying for *us*! They're either stupid or liars. Who wants to vote for any of them? If I knew voodoo, I'd pin a doll for those rotten bozos.

Victims' expression of personal, social, and political concern do not just articulate complaints. Solutions are proposed. In particular, interesting policy changes are posited by women who are homeless because of a lack of interest by politicians in following through with publicly proclaimed programs. Annie (age 60, Baltimore, Maryland, 1984) refers to one city's failure to fulfill assistance programs and offers specific suggestions:

> We had this big campaign to open shelters for battered women. All the politicians spoke out on how they were committed to assisting us. All we had to do was call the hotline number. We would get free legal help, and a place to live, and job training so we could start again. Guess what? No such thing. Oh, we had the number to call, and if we fit in we might get a chance at a bed in a shelter, but there wasn't no free legal help or any places to live, or real job training. I got into a shelter for a couple of weeks, and a nice lady told me I had to take pride in myself and get on with my life. The only free legal help was a TRO (Temporary Restraining Order), and I didn't need that; my man wasn't after me. He wanted to get rid of me! I needed a free divorce lawyer and access to our bank accounts, which he closed in my name. All that crap about job training? Someone offered me lessons in typing, and a ride to the unemployment office to look at the bulletin boards. At night the six of us at the shelter talked about how *we'd* help women like us. First, we'd make the politicians spend some time with us. They don't know the first thing about our problems, or if they do, they don't care. We'll tell them that instead of making a lawyer pay a fine for doing something, he should provide free services. Instead of making crooked builders pay fines or go to jail, they should put up buildings for the homeless or provide free apartments in the buildings they got. All them other white-collar crooks that end up in the courtroom? Let them spend some time in training us for real jobs instead of sending them off to some country club jail or fining them. Instead of telling our husbands to stop knocking us around and getting a few days in jail and a fine, let them feed us, buy us clothes, get us a job, pay for our medical bills, and get us a separate place to live. The politicians can't fool the victims, they only fool the people who don't need anything.

It is apparent from the many stories similar to Annie's that while most cities are proudly stating services for the abused and homeless, these promises are illusory. Sadly put by one author: "Failure better describes the lies society tells women about its ability to protect them. We tell women the orders of protection will save them from assaults. We don't tell them. . . that these orders will only save women if we print them on bullet proof material. We don't tell women that our courts have a poor record of punishing the men who violate orders" (Dowd 1991). State and local politicians become elected on platforms which offer hope for the general public, provide token programs, and create some very well-paid jobs for their appointees. Until one *needs* the services, as Annie points out, no one knows exactly what is available. Rachel (age 55, Philadelphia, Pennsylvania, 1979) also offers suggestions for positive change:

> I spent all day going from one public office to another. The State's Attorney sent me to the State Prosecutor. He sent me to the City Attorney's office. They sent me to the Attorney General's office. Then I was sent to the D.A. And all I wanted was the right to prove that my ex bribed a city official so that I couldn't get into court. Now that sounds wrong, doesn't it? Well, you just can't go to civil court without a lawyer, my friend. There aren't any free lawyers for us women who don't have money to hire anyone. I got to thinking about that. If we had a chance to tell the public about what happened, like in those public town meetings some places still have, and everyone in town knew what was going on, we'd get rid of the guys who just stick up for their pals. Now I'm not saying we'd get the right to slander people. No. They'd get the chance to answer our charges. But if we can prove what we are saying, there would be a hell of a lot less people out there who are only penniless, and a new kind of public official. They'd have to answer to the people who got screwed. Then the newspapers could publish their names. There isn't anything so good as advertising who did what.

I have heard many stories from abused (and now homeless) women who have discovered at various times in their relationships that they have married men who behaved in a similar fashion with other women. These men are recidivists: they commit the same type of act(s) on more than one victim. No one scholar has studied the recidivist spouse abuser. I consider such males as career criminals, perpetuating abuse and ruining lives throughout very long "careers" as marital con men (with or without legal vows). They are not only a matter of personal concern to individual women: they are also a matter of social and political concern. They prey on unsuspecting women, create new victims, and add to the community's expense. They are infrequently caught and/or punished; but when they are, the taxpayers must bear the cost of prosecution and incarceration. Upon release, these men tend immediately to resume their "careers." Their capture depends on the willingness of victims to testify about embarrassing circumstances, and that usually occurs when more than one woman has "told her story" about a particular man—and the victimization suggests bigamy or similar sensationalism. Since such stories make excellent newspaper copy, many women, having no desire to let others know of their misfortune(s), quietly divorce the offenders. The marital con game is not only a crime of victimization, but an experience which causes the victim to look a fool—and that deters discovery and elimination of recidivism. Margaret (age 34, Baltimore, Maryland, 1984) tells her story:

> I thought I was marrying the most sensitive man in the world. He was a widower with two young children, and he cried every time he talked about how these wonderful children had been tortured by a stepmother-bitch whom he had married two years prior to our meeting and left in outrage after only a few months of marriage. I saw the children spit at her in the grocery store, and heard constant references to her cruelty—which was always spelled-out in conjunction with the way she treated her own disabled child. I was especially touched by Richard's crying; somehow when he cried and asked for material things I never saw it as a deliberate attempt to get the money I had and he didn't. I was hurt when he refused to let the children call me "mother." He said he made that mistake with Bett-the-wicked-stepmother. I slowly heard a different story from Bett's friends. Richard had demanded money and a new house from her, too. He had made jokes about her in public. She had told friends of his private cruelties. He had continued a sexual relationship with his best friend's wife during his marriage to Bett. I had been the person who had broken-up his marriage to Bett! I floundered for excuses for him, always returning to his grief concerning his first, dead wife. I began to wonder

how she died. He began a merciless "teasing" campaign and I found myself crying in public. I subtly asked Richard's neighbors, acquaintances, bosses, and past dates about his personality. Everyone said he was absolutely charming when he wanted to be. Otherwise he was a calculating and money-grubbing bastard. His own mother would not comment on his past relationships. She had tried to dissuade me from marrying him, but I took it as an attempt to save *him*, not me. One day the woman he had been having an illicit affair with took me into her confidence. I'll never know if she did it to help me or just to get him back into her own devious clutches. Rich was out to get every woman he could, she had said. They were his way to financial success and an unpaid maid for him and his children. I knew that she was right. I took nine years of psychological and physical torture from him before I left and I didn't leave because I wanted to; I was thrown out after he threatened to kill me if I didn't leave without asking for anything. I had a choice of believing him or calling his bluff, and I had already seen his violence. It never seemed to let up. You know, he never once said he was sorry for anything he did to me, even to breaking my ankle. Boy, if I had known about his abusive past I never would have married him. He keeps his newest wife away from the rest of us. She'll never know we exist, poor woman.

Ann (age 39, Santa Monica, California, 1986) expresses a common fear regarding previous wives:

I dated Jerry for a year before we got married, and I knew that he had a pretty bad past. But none of it had to do with being violent to women. It was ADW[assault with a deadly weapon] and GTA [grand theft auto] stuff, and he was trying to make good when we were married. He began to hit me whenever he lost a job. He was okay when he was working. Then he started drinking and taking drugs. I blamed their effects for the beatings which followed. I was wearing sunglasses to hide black eyes, and limping most of the time. My own life was so full of fear that I couldn't think straight. I was ready to commit suicide. I really loved Jerry, and I didn't want to separate. There just had to be a way to reach him, I kept thinking, and I just wasn't coming up with it. Then one night we

were at a local bar and a girl came up to him and asked
about Tina. He pushed her away and made me leave with
him. I don't really know why, but I went back there myself
and after about a month I saw that girl again. We talked.
Jerry had had several live-in lovers which I hadn't known
about, and all of them had been molested by him. Broken
bones, rapes, strange car accidents where something had
been cut, and all kinds of terrible stuff. His few friends
never said anything to me, and if that girl in the bar hadn't
let me in on it, I would still think of Jerry as one sweet guy
with a drinking and drug problem. He's a public danger,
he is, and no one is doing anything about it. If a girl has
the nerve to tell on him to the police, she can forget having
any future. Tina did die eventually, and the autopsy said it
was an overdose. Tina's friends said she didn't take drugs.
Tina's friends also said that Jerry was still seeing her on
the sly while we were married. I'm scared to tell anyone;
you promise you won't use our real names? I just know I'd
end up dead too.

While I have not been attempting to conduct any statistical
studies on recidivism, the quantitative aspect of this problem
may be one of staggering proportions. As shelter support staff I
was constantly in contact with crisis-hotline callers and
residents. If the victim did not mention her abuser's past, I asked
about previous relationships; if I say that 75% of the women
recalled recidivist behavior, I may be understating the case. In
the city attorney's office, investigative reports and rap sheets are
attached to domestic violence cases; notable features are the re-
occurrence of narrative reports of past abuse and the filing and
conviction charges entailing Penal Codes 273.5 (spouse abuse)
and 242 (battery). In perhaps half of the cases the incidents relate
to the same victim. Upon talking to victims who have filed arrest
charges, I discovered that offenders have had one or more
relationships in which violence appeared as a major factor, and
there are no related police reports. Victims either do not think to
or are reluctant to offer information, but once on the topic of
abuse against women it is extremely common to come to the end
of a conversation with a history of repeated violence by the
offender. What I have been gathering is a psychography of males
who are career criminals in the area of domestic abuse. It
saddens me to report that when my ex-husband died in 1993, his

fourth wife contacted me. We never had any communication; in fact, I did not even know her name. I will not reveal the secrets she related about their relationship. But I will state that her concatenation of personal experience narratives contained the same contents of the stories I tell—which are rarely believed. It is interesting to note that the same attorney who supposedly befriended and then deceived me has done the same to her (see my upcoming personal narrative). Therefore it is not only the intimate abusers who are recidivists; it is also those who are in positions of power as attorneys or public officials.

There are salient reasons for women not reporting serious abuse to the police (aside from the reasons explicated elsewhere). "Family disturbance calls have been labeled the 'common cold' of police work. These calls. . . constitute the largest single category of calls received by police departments each year" (Mederer and Gelles 1989: 25). And yet, according to a major study, "only 10% [of women battered] called the police for help, apparently with good reason: almost all of the women who had called stated later that the police had provided absolutely no help at all. In fact, they often made things worse; once they were gone, after some feeble and ineffective attempts to placate the batterer and after the batterer saw that nothing had been done to stop him, he often continued his abuse with renewed violence" (Walker 1989: 63). This speaks directly to police attitudes and policies. "Arrest without coordination with other sanctions produced greater subsequent violence" (Gelles 1991). At the Women's Correctional Center in Chicago, "all of the women who had killed abusive mates reported that they called for police help at least five times before taking the life of the man; many said the violence they endured became more, rather than less, severe after their attempts at gaining assistance" (Browne 1987: 11). And the NCJA Justice Research study (1990: 3) reports that in nearly 50% of all homicides resulting from domestic violence in Newport News, Virginia, the victims had contacted police previously for help. To make matters worse, "the police are less likely to make an arrest if it is the victim who calls the police. They speculate that when the victim calls, the incident has not come to the attention of neighbors and other outsiders and, consequently, it is seen as less serious by the police" (Berk,

Fenstermaker and Newton 1988: 159). According to the Women
Against Abuse Legal Center in Philadelphia, about 2000 people
filed for protection orders [Temporary Restraining Orders] in
1989. In 1991, the figure was nearly 9000. As of 1992, the tally
was 25% higher (*Philadelphia Inquirer.* 1992). "The injuries that
battered women receive are at least as serious as injuries suffered
in 90% of violent felony crimes, yet under state laws, they are
almost always classified as misdemeanors" (Zorza 1989: 4). "The
conclusion drawn [from many studies] is that only a small
number of domestic violence cases ever result in conviction, and
those that do are subject to little post-conviction supervision by
the court" (Family Service of Philadelphia et al 1991: 7). There is
conflicting data regarding the newest police procedures and
policies. Some studies reveal insignificant change, no change, or
a rise in abuse despite police and public education and awareness (Hearings Before the U.S. Senate Judiciary Committee 1990;
Dunford, Huizinga, and Elliot 1990; Hirschel, Hutchison and
Dean 1992). Other studies find that more aggressive and
progressive police intervention effectuates better assistance for
the abused (Hotaling 1988; Walker 1989; Gelles 1991). The most
advanced policy-overhaul proposal cited is one urged by the
City Council of Los Angeles in response to the alarming number
of domestic violence emergency calls, prosecutions, and non-
prosecutions. In July of 1993, the Los Angeles Police Department
"began drafting a plan to link police prosecutors and nonprofit
agencies in a pilot program involving the notification of shelters
and counselors for battered women at the same time that officers
respond to a call" (*Los Angeles Times* 1993: B2). While I note the
positive aspects of attitude and concept, my belief is that it is
virtually an impossible pursuit! Can the reader envision such a
triumvirate act: the police entering "the unknown" of a domestic
violence house call while at the same time contacting a (usually
busy or "after hours"!) shelter number *and* a counselor? There
are only a few shelters in Los Angeles and they are unable to
handle the calls they already receive (let alone taking in the
battered women who wish assistance and housing), and to
which "counselors for battered women" does the Council refer?
The ones who work for the shelters are overwhelmed with their
current workload. Private practitioners do not do pro bono

counseling. W.O.A.H. (Women Organized Against Homelessness) is a nonprofit agency. Are the police now going to add to my volunteer efforts? In any case, there is nothing new to the link between the police and prosecutors; all police reports are passed almost immediately to the city or district attorney's office in which the prosecutors evaluate cases for arraignment or rejection. Even in the recent past it has been difficult to get officers interested in doing more than trying to "quiet" a couple; often the excuse has been made that it is simply a "domestic spat" in which there were mutual combatants. Women have been told to take a tranquilizer and try to "get along" with their husbands. Husbands have been told to "keep cool" and "take a walk around the block." In short, the police really did not take the matter of domestic violence seriously—certainly not as seriously as assaults in other categories. However, in the last two years some important strides have been made, with mandatory training sessions concerning domestic violence in many police academies, seminars in particular precincts, and a dedication by many city attorneys' offices to prosecute cases which were formerly rejected or dismissed. The unfortunate fact is that prosecutors by necessity are more interested in piling up statistics concerning the number of cases filed and offenders convicted in order to fit the ever-increasing yearly budget request than in what happens to the victim—who often needs more assistance after the battering as she faces "no place to go"—usually with no money, children to care for, and too often with no immediately marketable skills. Domestic violence victim advocates working in the court system are constricted by guidelines which prohibit assistance which I have heard termed "interference." I know because I was not allowed to provide the information, referrals, and personal contact which would have kept some women from becoming indigent and homeless as a result of a desired prosecution.

Police response is not the only—or even the most important—reason why women do not report domestic abuse. While many studies do note religious convictions, economic dependency and family pressure as variables in remaining with an abuser (e.g., Merrill 1989), I find, after listening to what victims say, that despite all of the other factors, economics is the ultimate determinant. Wealthy homemakers (finally) obtain (usually quiet) divorces in which they receive enough money to create a new home life, and working women with substantial incomes either devote more effort toward promotions or relocate to better jobs. It is the just-above-poverty-level, older, often disabled, unemployable woman and the younger parent with no decent wage-earning capacity who have the worst decisions to make: stay or leave with no real hope for a present and future.

What has not been accomplished? Finding and assisting 1) the abused woman who does not ever report domestic abuse to anyone, 2) the women who do prosecute and are left standing outside of the courtroom as their husbands go to jail, 3) the women whose husbands have been "diverted" to counseling groups in lieu of jail, and 4) the women who become indigent and homeless as a direct result of domestic abuse.

The discovery of pre-homeless women is the primary method of preventing indigency and homelessness. In order to effect such a complex task it is necessary to gain the assistance of public officials. They have the ability to see that every woman in need has the proper referrals and that all programs promised are present and productive. The operative word is accountability. It is crucial and sadly absent in our society. While I believe my informants' stories concerning officials in other cities, I can only prove the malfeasance in Baltimore, Maryland. My proof is in the form of letters from the officials in question, and court forms which contain misinformation. Many of my informants, given the opportunity, could also provide proof of unnecessary homelessness; however, I do not have the ability to be more than their voice in a publication. Therefore it becomes necessary to point to Baltimore as an example of a city creating homeless women as opposed to assisting them. What is more abhorrent than sad is that Maryland (and the National Organization for Women [N.O.W.], proudly and loudly laud Maryland's wide involvement in studying and deterring domestic abuse and adjunct homelessness. Between the Maryland-based Family Violence Coalition, the National Clearinghouse on Domestic Violence, the Special Joint Committee on Gender Bias in the Courts, the National Woman Abuse Prevention Project, N.O.W. chapters, the Domestic Violence Legal Clinic (under the auspices

of the House of Ruth [a shelter]), and several active victims'
rights coalitions, members have continuously and currently
testified in Washington, D.C. and presented papers at various
conferences (such as the American Society of Criminology held
in Baltimore in 1990) about the ongoing and increasing abuses
and deaths directly correlated to family violence. For example,
"In Maryland, about 16,000 cases of spousal assault were
reported in 1990. While this number is staggering, it reflects only
a fraction of the real number of incidents across Maryland. . .
most occurrences of family violence go unreported. Research
suggests, however, that the actual incidence is at least twice that.
. . . Even when [victims report abuse], only one jurisdiction out
of 24 requires written reports" (Family Violence Coalition: 1991).
In a 1989 study by the National Clearinghouse on Domestic
Violence in Rockville, Maryland, it was reported that "three to
four million females in intimate relationships are physically
beaten every year." (If that many women experience physical
violence, what does that suggest about emotional abuse?) The
Family Violence Coalition cites 70 Maryland women were killed
by their partners in 1990 (1991). It is not that system inadequacies
and failures are not brought out into the open; e.g., the Family
Violence Coalition in Maryland reported that "when funding is
available, it is often inadequate; . . . the Baltimore Zoo spent
twice as much money to care for animals as the State spent to
provide safety for women and children in all eighteen shelters"
(1991). However, no one in power seems to pay any attention to
all of the data and statistics; there is no accountability. The Bar
Association Grievance Commission (comprised of attorneys)
conducts sham (if any) investigations of victims' allegations
which protect their colleagues from disbarrment, local politicians
are loathe to make waves in the Old Boys' Network that works
so smoothly, and state officials deny responsibility, passing it
along until it disappears. Now if "town meetings" were an
integral part of every community's activities, accountability
would be enhanced with the enumeration of every offensive
behavior with names cited and then published in newspapers.
Everyone would have an equal opportunity to explain and the
public would be knowledgeable and ready for the next election.

While my story is unique to *me*, the essential details of victimization are not unique at all. I have over 150 stories of circumstances so similar that only names and places are interchangeable. Thirty-seven women in Baltimore County have shared stories naming the same names. I am the only one of those who is not living in a car, mall, shed, or temporary dwelling of decent sort. I have told my story orally so many times that I was intrigued by Lauri Honko's suggestion (at the Bergen meeting of the 8th Congress of the International Society for Folk Narrative Research, 1984) that folklorists record their own experiences so as to become both informants and observers. Honko interviewed himself on tape about long past events to test context and evaluate reconstruction and meaning. (His results were to be published at a later date.) I decided to try his suggestion to become an informant and observer, and this is what I "told" during my interview of myself:

> After several years of marriage to a man who bragged about his ability to psychologically abuse women, I was told to leave quietly or he would kill me and my son. He said that while holding a gun to my head. I agreed, of course, and as soon as I could I called his only friend— Joel—who was Rubin's business partner in some real estate deals. Joel is a lawyer, and when he saw what was happening, he took possession of the gun and promised to represent both of us so Rubin wouldn't get into trouble. I had a private appointment with Joel in his office the next day, and I believed he was my attorney. Anyway, Joel lied. He only meant to help Rubin and was making sure I didn't hire another attorney. Joel drew up separation papers which did indeed separate me from everything rightfully mine: home, personal belongings, furniture, stock, bank accounts, and alimony. He knew I was physically forced to sign the papers because I complained bitterly about his betrayal. His answer was that he could give the gun back to my husband if I wasn't satisfied, and he would say that he never promised me anything at all. I finally was just forced out of my house. I tried to find another lawyer. But I was then churchmouse poor, and hardly a desirable client. And I discovered that no lawyer wanted to cross Joel. I tried Legal Aid and they pleaded no funds! I filed a formal complaint with the Maryland Bar

Association's Attorney Grievance Commission concerning the gun and "promise," but that body refused to even ask Joel if he had the gun. Talk about corruption! They protected him, which may be a crime in itself. In any case, I persisted in trying to obtain legal assistance, and failed for several years. Finally, in 1981, my husband decided he wanted me back and began to call me every day for six months. I declined. I knew he treated other women badly and wouldn't change. So he called to brag that he had found a rich woman to marry. He filed for divorce, and I received notice of the trial date for April 12, 1983, from the Trial Assignment Officer for the Circuit Court of Towson, Maryland. Before I even had received my notice, which was dated January 25, 1983, my husband's attorney had written a letter which he hand-delivered to the trial assignment officer, Irene Summers, requesting a three-week postponement to accommodate his schedule (see EXHIBIT 1). She immediately granted that postponement request, and sent me another, corrected notice, dated January 31, 1983. I received both notices at approximately the same time, and then wrote to request a postponement for myself; I wanted time to prepare my own case, since I could not obtain a lawyer to represent me. The Assignment Office received my request on February 4, 1983—*after* Ms. Summers had already granted a postponement to my husband's attorney. On March 31, 1983, I received formal notice (as did my husband's attorney) that *I* would not be allowed a postponement because the previous postponement was given for the very same reason, and one can only have one postponement for the same reason (see EXHIBIT 2). That was a deliberate lie, of course, because the one and only postponement granted was to Mr. Nolan, for his convenience. I wrote to dispute the decision, and was ignored. I called and wrote to the Governor, the Attorney General, the State's Attorney, the State Prosecutor, the Criminal Justice Coordinator, the Human Resources Secretary, the Court Clerk, the Senators and Representatives, the County Executive, local council people, the ACLU, Legal Aid, the judges of the circuit court, Lawyers' Referral, the Bar Associations, and N.O.W.—both national and local chapters. Those who replied stated that someone else's office was in charge of such cases; no one seemed to be responsible for a crime

committed by a court officer. No one offered to help. I sent
a letter to the "Letter to the Editor" section of the *Baltimore
Sunpapers*, but it was not printed. The trial was held
without the victim—me—and the judge ignored the letter
which I can prove he received because my husband's
lawyer unintentionally noted it in correspondence. I filed a
formal charge with the Attorney Grievance Commission
against Stephen Nolan, who knowingly went along with
what he knew was a crime: a lie on a court notice. The
Attorney Grievance Commission refused to even ask the
attorney if he knew of the "error" on the court form. I
persevered; I kept on trying to reverse the illegally-held
trial by instituting another. Again I was—and still am—
ignored by every official and agency in Baltimore County.
What really hurts is that the State's Attorney and the
Criminal Justice Coordinator are women, and according to
the federal government, the State's Attorney's office is the
appropriate one to investigate. Sandra O'Connor has
refused to even answer my letters. Equally disturbing are
Criminal Justice Coordinator Connie Caplan's offer of
empathy (and nothing more), and the fact that the lawyers
of the Domestic Violence Legal Clinic, which is associated
with the shelter for battered women (the House of Ruth),
pretended that they were going to help me and then lied,
stating that the statute of limitations had run out. That lie
is easily proven by the dates of our letters and the date of
the final divorce decree. N.O.W., which is supposed to be
assisting women in gaining "equal rights," completely ignored my plea that the least their local members could do
would be to picket the courthouse where a man was
getting an illegal divorce and the court was creating an
indigent and homeless woman. If this could happen to me,
who has been able to correspond with all of the state
officials, the purported victims' rights groups, the law
schools in Maryland, every clinic available, and my own
senators in California, what chance does the ordinary
homeless woman living on the streets have in gaining
entrance to the court system to get what is morally and
legally hers?

Law Offices

NOLAN, PLUMHOFF & WILLIAMS
CHARTERED

J. EARLE PLUMHOFF
NEWTON A. WILLIAMS
WILLIAM M. HESSON, JR.
THOMAS J. RENNER
KENNETH H. MASTERS
STEPHEN J. NOLAN
WILLIAM P. ENGLEHART, JR.
JEAN M. SADOWSKY

204 WEST PENNSYLVANIA AVENUE

TOWSON, MARYLAND 21204

AREA CODE 301
TELEPHONE
823-7800

January 26, 1982

HAND DELIVERED

Ms. Irene Summers
Assignment Office
Circuit Court for Baltimore County
County Courts Building
Towson, Maryland 21204

Re: <u>Bard v. Bard</u>, Equity No. 111277

Dear Ms. Summers:

I received today a copy of the trial notice for the above-captioned contested divorce proceeding, scheduling the same for Tuesday, April 12, 1983 at 9:30 a.m. Due to a conflict, I am respectfully requesting that this case be rescheduled for a trial date on or after May 3, 1983.

I greatly appreciate your kind assistance in this matter.

Very truly yours,

Stephen J. Nolan

SJN:jka

cc: Marjorie Brook Bard

Mr. Rubin Bard

Form CA2

Jobl Adams — 494-2660
Civil Assignment Commissioner
Settlement Court

Maria Ercolano — 494-2662
Masters Assignment Clerk
Medical Records

CIRCUIT COURT FOR BALTIMORE COUNTY

ASSIGNMENT OFFICE
COUNTY COURTS BUILDING
401 Bosley Avenue
P.O. Box 6754
Towson, Maryland, 21204-0754
March 16, 1985.

Kathy Rushton — 494-2660
Assignment — Jury — Motions
Marcia Fennell
Assistant Clerk Typist

Irene Summers — 494-2661
Assignment — Non-Jury — Motions
Freddie Grove
Assistant Clerk Typist

TO: Stephen J. Nolan, Esq.

        M's Marjorie Brook Bard (P·)

        Note: Confirming notice that the above cited case remains
        in the assignment for trial on its merits for Tuesday,
        May 3, 1983, @ 9:30 a.m. Defendant's request for
        postponement has been denied due to the previous
        postponement was for the same reason, without
        variation.

RE: EQUITY - 111277 - BARD VS WARD

HEARING DATE: Tuesday, May 3, 1983, @ 9:30 a.m.

ON THE FOLLOWING: Merits: 1 hour

EXHIBIT 2. Denial of Marjorie Bard's postponement request
by Irene Summers on the grounds that the previous
postponement was requested by her and provided for her.

I discovered that I recalled dates, times, and people without error; if I am an example of an informant, then I have to trust my other informants. I discovered that my own narration brought to light answers to other questions I posed pertaining to victims' narratives. My story sounds "rehearsed." In fact, I have told myself that story (and others) so many times that I pay undue attention to specifics and sequence. I really do not know if that is a conscious maneuver or not. I sound authoritative. On the tape I hear frustration and anger in my voice. I hear those qualities in other victims' voices. The pitch and volume of my voice rise as the story unfolds; so do those of other victims. Perhaps the most intriguing factor is that there are practically no "ums" and "ahs" in the narratives. I have not deleted these from my documentation of my story or from the stories of other victims; they simply were almost non-existent. Our storytellings sometimes sound like educational films: instructional as opposed to entertaining. I analyze this aspect as the necessity for those who listen to believe in the events we characterize. Further, we apparently all feel that these experiences could happen to any woman, and therefore one must listen carefully to the details so as to be forewarned. We do not skip forward to the end; the effect is almost like a horror story in which one must build on each little event. Pertaining to this conscious or unconscious "strategy," Susan Stewart says (1981: 34):

> A hesitation in the narrative must be marked by the audience. There is no possibility of "skipping ahead" of the rattling of chains, or the wandering discourse of the letter—the audience is taken step by step through the text. To hear the ending of the tale first would be to cancel out the experience of it. There is little difference here between the structure of a text's temporality and the structure of the Fun or Horror House, where the victim is committed to experiences the full range of horrors presented and cannot simply jump out of the boat and swim back to the admissions gate or forward to the water chute that offers closure.

I also discovered that my storymaking is appropriate material for an oral historian. Perhaps the most important facts are those which pertain to the inadequacies of the proclaimed services of a community. Families and extended families have been taking care of many victims, providing the services that community social service agencies cannot provide. This is not unusual in itself, for "the family" is the most basic of organizations, and one which has universally provided "for its own" when society does not have suitable services. This most basic of organizations was created by a personal narrative: the marriage proposal. Victims of domestic abuse who become homeless often lose their first and most important organization—the family—and *must* turn to society for assistance. Unfortunately there are virtually no organizations which focus solely on female homelessness. In such cases, stories that may be revealed become the basis for the creation of *other* private sector support groups and larger, more permanent organizations which deal with associated personal, social, economic, and political issues. Andrew Pettigrew states (1979: 575):

> The analysis of organizational origins and uses and in particular their role in expressing communal values, evoking past experiences, providing seed beds for human action, and legitimizing current and evolving distributions of power represent key areas of inquiry in research on the creation and evolution of new organizations.

Organizational ethnology is the larger issue (and research project) of which the core is the ethos of individual organizations. "Ego" in ethnology refers to one who is the focal point in the study of organizational relationships. It is therefore propitious to study the individual(s) and the organizational ethos which springs from their efforts.

CHAPTER FOUR

Tell a Story, Start an Organization

Sally Evans of Cleveland, Ohio, explains why and how an organization was created (in a 1986 interview):

> There I was, sitting in the hospital bed with broken bones, hideous bruises, and a headache the size of Chicago. My only companion was a large paper flower that kept flapping from the slight breeze. It leaned toward me in a gruesome vase, probably from the hospital's occupational therapy class—you can't imagine how awful it was—and after three days I began to talk to it. That's how lonely I was. I told it how my husband had become furious just because I didn't have dinner ready on time. The flower, which I named Popsy, bobbed understanding and flapped away as if it were telling a story of its own. Boy, did we talk to each other a lot. I really wanted other women to talk to—you know, women going through the same kind of shit I was—but aside from the counseling group set up by the shelter there wasn't any place to go. I needed companionship with gals who had had similar kinds of shit and wouldn't think I was stupid or insane for staying so long, putting up with so much, and living with the shame, no, *disgust,* that I felt for letting myself become such a puppet. Do you know what I mean? [I nodded and murmured understanding.] About a week into my two-week stay I was walking down a hall and saw another woman looking as miserable as I was feeling. We both stopped to rest and started to chat. It took maybe fifteen minutes to get to the truth of the matter, but we shared a mutual, well, grief, I guess, that only those in our situation would understand. I could start a sentence and she would finish it. . . I asked her if she knew of any groups of women like us. She didn't and we both wanted an

organization which kept a steady membership of battered
and formerly battered women who met often and shared
the hurts and hurdles. Well, since there weren't such
organizations, we began to sound out women who we
either knew were being abused and weren't doing
anything about it, you know, trying to cover it up, or had
gone to shelters, or to court. They told us about other
women and we approached them, you know, very
discreetly and told them what had happened to us and
how we understood and how we thought getting together
would be beneficial to all of us in a meaningful way, and
well, we just set up a meeting, and it went great, and we
set up another meeting, and then regular ones, and F.A.B.
[Formerly Abused and Battered] was born. We had dinner
meetings at Beverly's or my house and it wasn't only great
to be together, but we came up with great ideas. We
formalized a plan to present to our state legislature to
allow women to go into a special courtroom without an
attorney to address a judge directly. It would have helped
women who had no desire to put their guy in jail but had
no income and just wanted the ability to become
independent. I moved about that time. My new husband
lived in Texas, and I admit that after about two months of
corresponding, I had other interests. [She looked ashamed
and began apologizing for her lack of continued
commitment.]

Was it just an accident that because two women had
similar experiences and consequent stories and exchanged
confidences that a subsequent *gathering* of people also with
similar experiences and stories occurred? Or, was it because
within each storytelling there was implicit or explicit expression
of organizing for a particular purpose?

That we can tell ourselves stories about traumatic events
has been established. It has also been noted that while we can
reconstruct characters and actions of a past experience into a
story which is told to self, that may not be sufficient. The story
may need to be shared with other people. Human interaction is a
normal function, and part of that interaction is in a conversational mode. It is natural that in response to specific cues
(verbal and nonverbal) from the one with whom one is communicating, a particular story may be elicited. In Sally Evan's

case, she "saw a woman who looked as miserable as she felt." She was drawn to her and communication began. One woman intuitively knew that she could speak to the other without reservation; one understood that another was in emotional distress, and that distress was shared. During the storytelling something else happened: a meeting of the minds occurred as to the nature of what each might say; i.e., they were sharing a thought pattern conceived in the experiences each encountered and which were so similar that one might have been the other's. In addition, explicit in their stories was that something should be done about the situations in which battered women find themselves. Action was needed. It would be necessary to find more women who were victims and organize to effect change. The only way to accomplish this goal was to tell their stories to other women and gather those who had similar experiences to explore shared problems and posited solutions. That group sharing evoked the desire for a more formalized commitment. An organization was created. It all began with one woman telling stories of her personal experiences to another woman.

The conception of a victims' rights organization can almost always be traced to a personal experience narrative. Those who have encountered the same abuses, the same frustrations in finding adequate assistance, the same feelings of isolation (and/or fear, sadness, anger, etc.), the same need to find others to tell their stories to, eventually discover compassionate listeners who share a goal to end that particular victimization— or at least to alleviate the injustices of its impact. The organization formed can be a small, on-going, and informal support group or have a large membership with formal meetings and very little personal input by the general membership. While there are significant differences, there are similarities which must not be overlooked: the parturient period of organizational development is comprised of the exchange of stories between victims, and nascence is demonstrated by a commitment to meet regularly, the memorialization of a philosophy and mission statement, the selection of "leaders" (usually but not always elected officers), and an agreement regarding community outreach. Personal experience narratives are an important part of the decision-making process. Dotty Andersen of Sherman Oaks,

California, relates how such stories are utilized in organizational creation (1986):

> I needed to talk with other victims of incest, but I was hesitant to join a group. I had an awful experience a year or so ago. I had just gotten to the point where I could acknowledge to myself that my father was a sick man whose desires ruined our family. I couldn't yet tell the world. I was watching a TV show which had victims of incest telling about their lives, and I decided to call the number given on the screen. I went to their next meeting, which was a healthy thirty mile drive. I didn't like the place where they met, a bank building meeting room. I didn't like the women. They were rather cold, aggressive, and treated me like a number. A "Hello, I'm Dotty" tag was plastered to my blouse. I didn't like the way they carried on the meeting; it was like a business conference. And they had donuts and instant coffee at the back of the room. It was a real turn-off. I didn't go back. So I suffered alone for another few months, and then a funny, well, odd, thing happened. I was standing in a grocery store line and heard a whispered conversation between two women in front of me. They were referring to an article in one of those checkstand magazines, and the word incest caught me. I don't know how I got up the nerve, but I followed one woman to the parking lot and asked her if she knew of any local groups for women just starting to work through this problem. She was wonderful to me. I ended up at her house the next week. There were five of us, all neophytes to talking in public about the multiple problems facing us, and we spent several hours sharing our fears, and crying, and eating. The next week another woman joined us. She brought someone else the next time we met. We decided to make it a weekly potluck dinner and keep our group to no more than twenty. It's been great. We have a charter now and let me tell you, we all told horror stories of experiences in other groups as we made up our own rules for D.V.O.I. [Defiant Victims of Incest]. We got rid of all the negative traits that came up and emphasized all of the positive traits that we found in other group experiences.

I considered how folklorists have investigated the relationship between storytelling and the conscious selection of

time and place for sharing stories. The planning and maintenance of such storytelling groups would be tantamount to
"organizing" for individual and collective benefits. In studying
the storytelling sessions at the La Have Island general store,
Richard Bauman revealed that the men of the island had need of
a *continuing* source of pleasure and inspiration; they set a
particular time and sought a particular place to tell stories and
excluded women and children from their sessions; i.e., they
created boundaried setting for themselves. They had organized
and perpetuated what had been needed and successful. Their
lives benefited directly from the sessions. Bauman says (1972:
330-343):

> The gatherings at the store represented an occasion in
> which the display, maintenance, and development of
> personal identity was of paramount importance, through
> the exploitation of a conversational resource in personal
> terms. . . . The sessions at the store represented a forum in
> which this information could be exchanged. They afforded
> the participants a continuous opportunity to engage in
> personal and social identity-building by presenting the
> self in personal narrative and receiving like accounts about
> others in the same form. . . . This contributed to
> establishing and validating his social identity,
> membership, and status within the group. . . . The sessions
> at the store [also] constituted a forum in which wisdom
> could be shared, and safe, proper, and productive
> reactions to situations and forces that any member of the
> group might potentially encounter could be shared.

In essence, that which the men created was a support
group in which they could share mutual joys and concerns
without fear of judgment by "outsiders." The communitas which
is a necessity among the dependent islanders is metaphorical
and analogous to the situation in which isolated victims seek
psychological support and wisdom from those who offer an empathetic ear and advice in the closed, i.e., boundaried, setting of
a support group. Fellowship, or sociability, is inherent in the La
Have Island general store sessions; the men tell personal stories
and listen to others'. They tell jokes which might be completely
misunderstood by men outside of their group. So it is with the
victims who gather to tell their personal and third person stories

in a support group which may be the only means of fellowship available. Coleen Davis founded a chapter of Parents of Murdered Children. She explained to me how her organization was created (1987):

> My husband accused me of over-reacting during the two and a half years of investigation, arrests, trial, and sentencing hearing. He kept his feelings to himself. Our marriage ended and our other son was too stunned to talk about the tragedy until he managed to write some powerful poetry about his brother and the murder. What happened to my son when he was down in that canyon? What agony did he suffer and what fear haunted him during those days? I re-lived what could have happened over and over again. I sought help from general victims' assistance groups, but the only thing that made a difference in coping with my loss was being with others who were grieving from the same kind of experience. I started to pull these parents together to share; that's the only way to survive—with others who have gone through it. In the group we can talk. We can plan. One continues to seek a meaning in life. The best I can hope for is to be constructive. In 1984 our group linked with the national organization of Parents of Murdered Children, and since then I have organized Children of Murdered Parents. These kids of all ages need to work out their feelings too; the children and our P.O.M.C. group meet twice a month as a support group, once at a restaurant and the other at my house for a potluck brunch. The adults used to meet in a church, but we decided that we had to have more intimate surroundings. So we now meet in a living room with good food and good talk. It makes the members feel more at ease so they can bring out their worst fears and concerns. Every time a story was told about the murderer involved in one of our cases being freed, the subject of needed legislation would come up. Since P.O.M.C. is nonpolitical and I wanted to take a stronger stand, I shared my story with other victims who had similar experiences and goals. I began another organization, the Coalition of Organizations and People (CO-OP), which I mean to be a networking organization leading to legislative reform.

Sociability in its "getting together to talk" sense usually includes refreshments, especially if the session is intended to last for more than two hours. I wondered why there was no mention of particular snacks or potables accompanying "talk" at the evening-long sessions at the La Have Island Store. I cannot imagine men spending hours telling yarns, exchanging news, and arguing around a pot-bellied stove on stormy nights without some favored brew or homemade food being consumed. If Bauman's islanders never mentioned the inclusion of food (or if he simply ignored such mention because it appeared to be insignificant to his study), I could not ignore my informants' constant references to the need for and enjoyment of food and drink at initial meetings in which personal stories were shared, and within the scope of maintaining organizational ambiance. Whether it has something to do with keeping one's hands and mouth busy so as not to be idle ("I didn't know what to do with my hands; they just lay there in my lap waiting for a dishrag"), or whether eating abates nervousness ("My mouth was either going to be full of dumb words that obviously belonged to someone else or cake"), or whether the sensory stimuli of food satisfies unconscious desires ("That *smell*! It was better than any sex with Randy!"), refreshments of some kind are traditionally part of intimate gatherings. Linda Humphrey's study of "small group festive gatherings" delineates the ways in which food serves as a cohesive mechanism: it "imparts a sense of community, of belonging, and of intimacy" (1979: 198). Essentially, that is what victims' support groups are: small group festive gatherings, on the level of sustained meetings such as Humphrey's "soup night," which has met nearly every Thursday for years for the purpose of fellowship, or sociability. Humphrey emphasizes that storytelling is an integral part of the sociability. She does not limit the word "festive" to joyful occasions; she recognizes that family auctions and funerals are occasions at which people gather for a purpose and food offers a means to share, or comfort, or gladden. Food certainly offers a means to conversation, and conversation more often than not leads to someone telling a story of a personal experience.

Donuts and instant coffee waiting on a folding table in a rented room in a bank building do not have the same effect as a potluck brunch at someone's house. The woman who is interested in courting new members to a proposed organization which depends on the sharing of intimate life details will be sensitive to the need for making everyone feel completely comfortable. If the initial group does not return, there will be no opportunity to further the cause. People need to be persuaded to attend regularly, and while personal experience narratives may create an initial gathering so as to exchange sad or glad tidings and socio-political concerns, fellowship is significantly enhanced by the traditional behavior of sharing food. Storytellings, fellowship, sociability, food, and drink all add up to a continuing membership, and that is how many organizations function optimally. It is how organizations founded by victims for the purpose of sharing stories and pursuing activism on behalf of the members (and other victims as well) succeed where others often fail.

We have, therefore, the initial storytelling between "selves" which is the natural order of memory reconstructing noteworthy events and which is a rehearsal for telling stories to others; there is the need to tell others of similar circumstance about one's personal experiences; once shared, the stories circulate among those who will be interested; parties who no longer desire isolation but are in need of fellowship or advice seek similar others; those who have leadership in mind persuade others to join forces by the re-telling of the most egregious of experiences; and membership is cultivated and maintained by sociability blended with activism.

Oral storytelling is the most pervasive and persuasive means by which to initiate an organization of and for victims. There is also, however, hardly such an organization which does not have a brochure which boldly presents the origin of the group. The personal experience narrative of the founder is attention-getter and membership solicitor. It is as close to face-to-face communication as one can get when initial personal interaction simply is not possible. The brochures are personalized not only in story format, but in symbolism: the teardrop, for instance, is used extensively—alone or in conjunction with a flower ("The Weeping Rose") or a child's innocent face. Clasped hands and intertwined fingers symbolize the fellowship offered.

What surprised me was that some of the "organizations" represented by brochures were not really formed yet; the brochures were the work of one or two people (usually women) who were either geographically isolated, or unsure as to how to approach a new and sensitive issue, or had had no success in attracting membership. The brochures are mailed to prospective members or displayed on the tables available at conferences or conventions for victims' rights groups. The (written) personal narrative is used to entice an interested party to contact the brochure-author with a story of her own in the hope of creating a viable organization through the mail. When a membership is so encouraged, a meeting will be planned in which individuals will gather for face to face interaction. Consequently, when there is no other choice but to resort to printed material, personal stories directed to those whose experiences are similar and whose stories are often as yet untold, is a method of creating a specific type of organization.

Victims' rights organizations are created because personal concerns are also collective concerns, i.e., there is a dominating concern which overwhelms all. Those who share specific backgrounds—especially traumatic or unusual ones—share thought patterns which emanate from those experiences, and those thought patterns become themes which are structured into narrative form. Each person brings his own repertoire of similar themes to a particular group whose members are *expected* to be empathetic because each person completely understands why others are present. This aspect of expectation is important, for if someone tells a story and the theme is recognized, all that is needed is to correlate a theme with a personal experience and address the relevant experience to the preceding narrative. Referring to the isolated and dependent La Have islanders, Bauman notes of their storytelling (1972: 337):

> These individual contributions were bound together by a chain of association, a process in which each yarn was elicited by association, through some sharing of a common ground, with the preceding one. . . .An informant explained the dynamic thus: "some feller would tell a yarn, and by the time he was finished the next one would

have one that led off of it—something that he had heard or saw."

It is not even necessary for a teller to complete a tale before another attempts to introduce his own experience. Susan Kalčik refers to the germ of a story or a reference to a theme as a "kernel" story (1975: 7),

> which is a potential story, especially if the details are not known to the audience. . . . [or] may not be developed beyond this kernel if the audience already knows the story and an allusion to it is considered sufficient or if the kernel is offered by way of a supportive comment, indicating that the narrator has had a similar experience to one being presented by someone who has the floor.

Kalčik attributes this ability to continue a story referred to or in progress to women only, as their unique manner of response to "the rhythm of women's lives" and as a distinctive narrative structure (1975: 11). I would expand that ability to any group with a common repertoire and understanding. The group perceives similar imagery, and it is not *women* who have created a unique story structure, but rather any twosome or group which shares perception. Donald Ward calls this a shared perceptual paradigm (1979). He illustrates the concept by remarking on Thomas Kuhn's (1962) reference to members of a highly trained scientific community (1979: 261):

> Each member. . . shares a set of implicit assumptions about reality with other members of the scientific community. These shared sets of assumptions enable scientific specialists to communicate ideas to one another with maximal economy and efficiency but, at the same time, they serve to cut off communication with those who do not share these sets of assumptions. The communication is thus possible only when the two parties share the same perceptual paradigm. . .I suggest that this paradigm of perception need not be limited to the process of communication among specialized scientists. The paradigm is crucial in all forms of human communication and especially in the case of the performance and perception of art forms. Each person perceiving an artifact of performance (alloperform) brings with him the totality

of his experience and education which influences the paradigm.

Hence, victim support groups which are specialized (e.g., incest or spouse abuse) provide an immediate resource of individuals with similar experiences and related stories. The moment a personal narrative is begun, the teller expects her audience to understand exactly what her purpose will be, her emotions are, and in general, what her story will be about. The group will not, for example, be confused as to her subject matter or motives for narrating such a personal story; they will share assumptions about "their" reality and can communicate within the same perceptual paradigm. "Meaning," states Ward, "must be understood as being an integral part of the entire performance and perception situation" (1979: 263). In other words, the members of a victims' group (much as Bauman's islanders) who are sharing intimate details through storytellings have an expectation of what will be told and understand what is meant without explanations which would be necessary to "outsiders." The group metaphorically has a built-in radar system.

A victims' support group is really a collection of personal experience stories; with the advent of formalization, such an organization can become nationally recognizable. Mothers Against Drunk Drivers (MADD) is such an organization; it was created from personal stories and is so well known that no one has to explain its founding. Not so widely recognized is the Sunny von Bulow National Victim Center. It originated with the personal narratives of Ala Kneisel and Alexander von Auersperg, the children of (former Princess) Sunny von Bulow, who is in an irreversible coma. The highly publicized trials of (stepfather) Klaus von Bulow as alleged attempted-murderer finally resulted in his acquittal, but Mrs. von Bulow's children remain adamant that they were powerless victims of a system which provided excessive leniency to the accused. Vital issues, according to the victim-children, are those that are often espoused by other victims, namely that victims are not afforded the same privileges as are offenders, and that legislative reforms are necessary and will only come about by coalition-building and activism.

Such large organizations serve functions that the smaller grassroots support groups and organizations cannot perform: they provide a clearinghouse for (national) referrals and offer grants for specific projects.

As has been illustrated, just telling a personal story may result in the formation of an organization. The personal experience narrative has further functions in intraorganizational usage. The next chapter will examine the role of such stories as strategy in crisis situations.

CHAPTER FIVE

Personal Narratives as Intervention Strategy in Intraorganizational Crisis

Personal narratives which have been told to others of similar experience or concern often lead to the formation of an organization which becomes an established part of a community. Such organizations may include shelters for battered women or runaway minors; residential programs for alcoholics, drug addicts, the mentally ill, or the developmentally disabled; and facilities for the housing (and often job training) of homeless men or women. These organizations may be staffed by victims and ex-victims and continue to be self-sufficient within private sector funding, or continue to be considered as private sector, grassroots organizations but apply for and receive public sector monies and thus lose autonomy, or gradually become part of the public sector network with funding and personnel completely independent of any original membership or intent. In all of these organizations, crises will occur in some form; however, it is within the small, private sector organization which has come to rely on some public sector funding in order to continue operation that internal crises can be most destructive. It is often necessary for such an organization to solve internal problems without external assistance since any public knowledge of the crisis may actually threaten the existence of the organization.

I will present a case study of an organizational crisis which did dictate internal intervention. The intervention strategy utilized was the telling of personal experience narratives, at first purposefully by a support staff member (me) and then by those residents who, responding to me and my story, shared their pertinent stories in a continuing feedback and response situation.

The organization was—and I assume still is—comprised of six distinct groups of individuals. Four of these six perform in a hierarchal management capacity, and the other two are the very reason for the existence of such an organization: the resident clients. The crisis was precipitated by an accident. Those lowest in power in the hierarchy (the clients) sought to capitalize on the situation, their actions threatening to disrupt the organization, thwart the goals and objectives of the institution, and subvert their own best interests. Although it was apparent to many that the organization was on the verge of dissolution, no one seemed able to stop what was happening. The sudden and severe crisis necessitated an immediate and internal intervention. Leadership was totally involved in a negative and paralyzing situation. I was in a particularly advantageous position to intercede; I was in the middle of the hierarchy, relatively new to the organization, and as a volunteer, I was expendable. Although my behavior was viewed initially by the most powerful in the organization as dysfunctional, my intervention tactics proved to be effective in counteracting the destructive forces that had been unleashed.

The eastern facility is a not-for-profit organization established to aid homeless women and their children. It competes with similar organizations for public sector funding, and is heavily dependent on private sector donations. The shelter's converted two-story office building is on a small, narrow lot. A once-paved rear parking area is now a fenced yard with flower and vegetable gardens, benches, and playground equipment. The facility contains both a large staff office and a residential unit for the homeless women and children.

Life within the confines of this limited environment constitutes a well-defined social system: close interpersonal relations develop in and revolve around the sharing of the kitchen and the bath, dining, and living rooms. Staff and residents also share the tasks of cleaning, shopping, laundering, and gardening. They are in close proximity most of the hours of a twenty-four hour day; both staff and residents adhere to "house rules" to facilitate and ensure the continued functioning of the organization. Staff members, of course, follow the strict regime by choice rather than necessity.

While firm friendships often develop among staff members (who share similar upper-middle class backgrounds), the differences in cultural, ethnic, religious, economic, educational, and social backgrounds of the residents—as well as their transiency—result in "guarded bondings" between them. Disagreements are neither uncommon nor unexpected. Resident attitudes toward the staff are, in general, based on dependencies, and "friendship" is not necessarily desired or easily attainable. Communication and interaction are selective and intermittent, usually in one-on-one or small group situations. The hierarchy of power and privilege in the shelter is as follows:

1. The salaried, full-time facility staff
2. The hourly-paid, part-time facility staff
3. The veteran volunteers
4. The new volunteers
5. The women residents
6. The children

Each staff member works an eight-hour shift five days a week; there are three shifts each twenty-four hour periods. The night and Sunday staff members have a "special" image: they are viewed as "socially" important in contrast to the day workers (who are seen as more "business-like" or aloof) because their roles involve children's bedtime activities and the traditional Sunday outings. The hourly, part-time staff members have shorter, irregular shifts, but they work a seven-day week. The veteran volunteers have regular shifts of three four-hour periods a week. The new volunteers are committed to three three-hour shifts a week until a five-month training period qualifies them for veteran status. First choice of shift hours comes with "vet" standing. "Vets" often graduate to paid positions.

There are always four to seven families (women with children) in residence. They rarely enter or leave at the same time, and are allowed to remain at the facility for three months to attend job training workshops and counseling sessions, and pursue a continuous search for employment and affordable housing. Thus, while the staff remains relatively stable and constant, the women and children do not. The diversity of the clientele adds to the strain of daily intimacy in which several families with differing needs have to share communal living quarters *and* interact on a client-counselor basis with the organizational staff. The private or personal space of each resident woman is limited to a small bedroom which is frequently invaded by wandering children. Personality conflicts among the residents are mitigated only by a common realization: they need a place to live regardless of the impositions and inconveniences.

While the organization outwardly appears bureaucratic, there is among the staff a genuine caring for people and a commitment to assist those in crisis and transition. The paid staff accepts a much lower salary than their education and experience could command elsewhere. Job satisfaction is based on dedication, pride, and exaltation in each achievement. Such satisfaction also reduces conflict among all personnel and provides strength in confronting the constant threat of the dissolution of this much-needed facility. In addition, their "clock world" allows them to escape to another lifestyle, making possible their continued commitment to an impossibility: eliminating homelessness.

At the time of the crisis, four women were in residence with a total of thirteen children ranging in age from infants to a fourteen year old boy. Carol (Anglo) and Maria (Puerto Rican) had been at the shelter for five weeks and had formed a tenuous friendship based on a mutual love of cooking what they conceived to be "gourmet meals." The staff encouraged them, although their idea of haute cuisine was dramatically different. Mealtimes were often trying experiences because staff was almost always invited—and hence expected—to participate. Deni (Black) had arrived two weeks before; she felt alienated, which she attributed to racial discrimination. Geraldine (Native American and Anglo) had been in residence for only one week. She was quiet and prayed constantly with her tightly-held beads.

All of the women were trying to cope with purely personal problems and those originating in interaction with each other, the staff, and the volunteers. Two days before the crisis, Deni and Maria discovered a common interest in the occult and began long, private talks in a corner of the yard, leaving Carol alone. She became increasingly sullen. Geraldine encouraged her to pray, a suggestion Carol rebuffed ungraciously. Everyone was aware of the mounting tension, which was discussed at the (regular) weekly house meeting. The women grew more aloof from each other and the staff; it was rumored among them that one of the residents had secretly complained to staff about another serious matter. Then the crisis occurred—an accident that could have been fatal. (The need for anonymity prevents describing the incident; suffice it to say that it happened to Maria and two of her children, and there were no injuries.)

The residents banded together, blaming the full-time staff for the incident. The women as a group marched into the office and announced that they were going to sue the facility. They had prepared their grievance; they could foresee "millions of dollars" in a settlement from "an insurance company."

Maria assumed the role of victim. Carol's sullenness lifted as she donned the mantel of Maria's advocate. And Geraldine—the pious, patient, and passive housemate—turned openly hostile to all except her comrades.

The residents had assumed positions of authority, threatening the formal leadership and even the very existence of the facility. For the next four days, the full-time staff was disoriented and defensive, lacking control over everyday events; members were preoccupied with blame-placing, personality conflicts increased, and the sharing of the workload suffered significantly. Further, each resident had been assigned an advocate upon arrival; that staff member acted on the resident's behalf in all important matters. With the sudden turn of events, a dilemma was created: the advocate did not know whether to defend the residents or protect the facility.

Confusion reigned. The children—the most vulnerable group in the organization, and having the least authority or control—sensed a breakdown in leadership. They became aggressive and assertive in regard to bedtime hours, eating outside of designated areas, outings, and access to the sacred office space of the staff (perhaps the most crucial symbolic expression of power). The leader who emerged as the voice of the normally least-empowered group was Bob, the fourteen year old, a youth who deeply resented his position in the facility as neither "child" nor "adult." He gathered the other children into a cohesive unit to take advantage of the situation as well as to perpetuate it; for without a concerted effort to gain attention or "perks," they would have no control at all. Moreover, without the dissension among the elders of *all* groups, the children would have no opportunity to enter the arena of power.

The mothers seemed pleased and amused, at least initially, by the staff's lack of control over the situation, and approved the mischief of the children who were becoming increasingly ingenious in their disruptive behavior. The power and privilege hierarchy in the facility had changed drastically.

1. The women residents
2. The children
3. The new volunteers
4. The veteran volunteers
5. The hourly-paid, part-time facility staff
6. The salaried, full-time facility staff

The volunteers have always been rather a neutral force in the facility. Their turnover rate is significantly higher than that of the staff, and, for paraprofessionals, "volunteer" authority is always subordinate to staff authority. Gaps in duties also create spare-time periods. Because of their neutrality (or position in the middle, and hence potential as mediators), they respond to other groups in varied ways. They interact with the children, mothers, and full-time staff on the basis of individual relationships and in response to the immediacy of a situation. They are often a buffer in the interactions between parent and staff. However, the "vets" among the volunteers, who outrank the newcomers in seniority, are perceived variously. To the staff, long-time volunteers are viewed as either agreeable or ingratiating, or needed because of a particular skill (e.g., art therapist); to the new volunteers they are tutors; and to the residents they are closer to themselves than the staff but closer to staff status than the new volunteers.

During the onset of the crisis not all of the volunteers were aware of what was happening, for they are present intermittently and for a short span. It was not long, however, before they became aware that their status was changing. They were no longer in a buffer zone, but had greater authority than the staff. Someone had to enforce the essentials of housekeeping, and the mothers and children deferred to the volunteers. The staff was then forced to view the volunteers as more than "helpers." The fact that the volunteers were only implementing policy and not creating it made no difference: the mothers and children listened to the volunteers with new respect while snubbing the staff. The more recent the volunteer, the greater the influence, because the "vets" were more closely identified with the staff. The self-esteem of many volunteers rose; but they realized that this was a temporary situation and that their behavior would be evaluated by staff afterwards. It was a double bind for the volunteers.

The regular bi-monthly meeting of selected staff and all volunteers occurred four days after the crisis began. The staff was clearly distraught and tried to maintain control over intragroup and intergroup relationships but without much success. Although everyone realized that cohesiveness was needed, roles had shifted so drastically that long-subordinated personal conflicts surfaced. No one in a leadership capacity was coming forth to interpret properly and intercede. I had been a participant since the first day of the crisis, had changed my shift hours to ensure that I was present every day, and had been taking notes. I was able to detach myself enough to determine that I was the only likely interventionist. Staff members were already using the volunteers as scapegoats: everything that had been ignored or handled incompetently by the well-meaning volunteers was "not staff's fault." Unfortunately, the staff was and is responsible for the continuance of the facility, and the single fact is that almost without exception, the volunteers are expendable. It was imperative that the hierarchy of power and privilege among the groups be restored; the new power of the homeless women was dysfunctional to them as well as to the organization whose very assistance they sought. Disaster was imminent.

If I offered to be a mediator—presenting an ethnography of the situation and assisting others to articulate the problem and possible solutions—my role as a volunteer in the organization might be compromised. I did not wish to alter my persona.

I further rearranged my shift hours so that I could be on hand daily, using the excuse that I was going on vacation soon and was simply "making up my time beforehand." The morning after the disturbing staff-volunteer meeting, I entered the shelter and committed the unthinkable: I accepted the (unusually) gracious offer of the residents to share their homemade muffins and freshly-brewed coffee. The residents knew that this would irritate the staff, and ordinarily I would have politely declined and gone directly to the office to commence my duties. I sat down with the women at "their" table. They inferred from this act and my general demeanor that I was "on their side." My sharing food and space at the table reserved for the mothers provided a contextual advantage: *their* status seemed to prevail. We needed to share more than space, however; proximity alone would not endow acquiescence to the subtleties of persuasion and negotiation that I was planning. I awaited a topical similitude: an opportunity to tell of a personal experience relevant to those of my audience. (I was familiar with the data in their files.) Maria was decrying "the system," characterizing an incident in which she was evicted from her apartment and was forced (with her children) to live in a park—and was harassed by police and social workers. While she was narrating, she became increasingly aware of me as a person. She scrutinized my clothing, jewelry, handbag, and even a shoe that was in view—and apparently judged that I could not possibly understand her situation. Her story came to an obviously-foreshortened halt; she was receiving negative feedback from my presence and responded accordingly. The other women had noted Maria overtly evaluating me; and the three suddenly became absorbed in buttering muffins or pouring coffee. Maria continued to stare at my necklace. There was dead silence for a moment.

I reached out to put my hand over Maria's. I felt her fingers tense, but she did not draw away. I spoke earnestly:

> Maria, not so long ago my husband threatened to kill me if I didn't get out of our house so he could be alone with his teen-aged daughter. He had a gun and a knife, and I knew he was violent. I'd had so many years of abuse that I knew I had to do as he said or I'd be dead. He would have found a way to make it look like a suicide. I called the only person I could trust, but there wasn't anything she could do. So I drove to the nearest police station and told the really bored officer what had happened. I was given a couple of tranquilizers and told, "When you're shot, we'll investigate." They suggested I hire a lawyer. If I'd had the money for a lawyer, I wouldn't have been crying in a police station!

The women nodded and murmured in agreement. I received positive feedback through their facial expressions, intent listening, and forward-leaning bodies. I went on with my tale:

> I had no place to go, so I called every agency in Baltimore, assuming there would be all kinds of assistance available. There certainly had been lots of publicity about the development of such programs. But all I got were excuses or rudeness, and advice to hire an attorney or to tell the police. I was panicky and just started to drive. I parked in hotel and shopping center lots, used public bathrooms [The women again murmured in empathy. Geraldine said, "Amen."], and three days later I found myself in Maine. I was wandering, got lost, and discovered a small, deserted island where I spent the next several months.

Maria's hand had relaxed under mine; she, Geraldine, and Carol were still absorbed in my story. Deni, in the other hand, had shifted in her chair; her eyes were on her coffee cup, which she kept turning on a pattern in the tablecloth. I noted that negative feedback and paused. Without looking at me, Deni stated coldly and bluntly, "You're white. You've got a college degree. You could have walked into any job—or the N.O.W. headquarters—or the governor's office, for that matter. We don't get past certain doors." I saw Carol open her mouth to say something, but Deni continued rapidly. "Everyone who runs this place is white, or haven't you noticed?" Carol looked uncomfortable; after all, she was white. Geraldine and Maria were startled; they glanced at each other and then into space. Maria's hand slipped from under mine. She, Deni, and Geraldine made movements indicative of leaving the table. I knew I could lose my audience as quickly as I had gained it; I saw my storytelling-tactic faltering. "You're different," Deni muttered.

I responded quickly:

> Okay; you're right about our all-white staff and volunteers. But we certainly can't force minorities to work here. It's not a matter of discrimination. But you're wrong about my being different. I'm a woman. I was terrorized by a bully and refused assistance by police, the Criminal Justice Coordinator, and social workers. When I sat in that

car—with no home to return to—I was just like any of you.
I wasn't considered a first-class citizen. As for the job,
well, frankly, all I knew about were the kinds of jobs
where you set up an appointment in advance, have a
formal interview, and await a decision. I had no
experience with anything immediate or temporary—or
physical. And doors were closed to me too, Deni. I was
turned down by Legal Aid, and when I walked into a
lawyer's office, he nearly laughed at me. I obviously
couldn't pay his fee, and what I told him meant a
malpractice suit against a fellow attorney, probably one he
knew socially. He did tell me that I ought to file a
complaint with the Maryland Attorney Grievance
Commission, but he was smirking when he said it. I did
though, and the Commission lawyers refused to even ask
the attorney if or why he had the gun used on me. When
my husband filed for a divorce, another attorney
conspired with a court officer to rig a quick-and-dirty
trial—and lied in order to prevent me from being in the
courtroom. The Attorney Grievance Commission didn't
see any reason to question him about that.

Carol had been awaiting a chance to participate, tapping
her fingers on the table and opening and closing her mouth.
Finding the opportunity she wanted, she hastily began to
narrate.

My sister-in-law had the same kind of experience. She
filed charges against a lawyer, and an Attorney Grievance
Commission chewed *her* out for making what they called a
"bald allegation." The "bald allegation" was born six
months later, looks just like the lawyer and inherited a
rare genetic disease which runs in his family. [She
continued with a long story about the woman's problems
with public agency workers.] Without money or
connections, a woman is still a slave!

"How come she didn't go to N.O.W. for help? Or you,
Marjorie?" Geraldine's facial expression contained a measure of
compassion, but her tone was suspicious.

Carol shrugged and made a face. "As far as I'm concerned,
women libbers are women fibbers. I paid dues to N.O.W. for
years, but all I ever saw them do was run or march for E.R.A.

Shit; the Constitution already gives us 'equal rights.' We just can't use them!"

I knew I could add a story to that theme and thereby return to the storytelling session to pursue "our-organization-as-a-necessity."

> I did go to the N.O.W. office—after I had called repeatedly and was given a run-around. A staff member told me that N.O.W. doesn't assist individuals. Then she pointed to women sitting on the floor making signs and said I should join them. They were preparing for an E.R.A. march. I told her I needed immediate help as a victim, and the women insisted my only hope was to donate money to N.O.W. to ensure the E.R.A. passage. I yelled at her that another piece of paper wasn't going to help a victim who couldn't even find a lawyer to represent her—and what I needed was a place to stay, with people who shared my problems, cared about *doing* something about them, and could offer solutions.

Carol turned to Deni. Her expression was stern, her tone bold.

> I'm white. You know what I've been through. I was shoveled from the unemployment office to social workers to Legal Aid to welfare. And all the while I lived with any man who'd put us up for the night and feed us. What I haven't told you is how I got these. [She pulled up her skirt to show burn scars on her thighs.] I tell anyone who sees them that a kitchen fire caught me. A man who promised to keep me and the kids safe got his kicks this way. I begged the police to arrest him. I begged a Legal Aid lawyer. I begged a social worker. Everyone either passed the buck or told me to leave him. But that meant living on the street. No one offered job training, housing, food, clothing, medical treatment, or counseling. A prostitute saw us crammed in a phone booth trying to keep warm, and she gave me this number. I got a *chance* now. I really needed the counseling group. I can see now that my screaming at the kids is my way of screaming at myself. I need lots of help—and I'm getting it here.

She began to cry. Geraldine handed her a tissue and picked up her rosary, speaking rapidly in Spanish. When she saw our confusion, she laughed. It broke the tension. She sighed heavily.

> I guess our problems aren't so different. I got a job as a waitress, but I was so scared that Renaldo would find me that I kept dropping dishes and mixing up orders. I got fired from two jobs in a row. I had to move our things to a car in a vacant lot. The police told social welfare, and a lady came to tell me she would take my kids away. [She looked directly at Deni.] She was Puerto Rican or Cuban; she told me in Spanish that I was filth to let my kids live in a car. But she didn't offer to help me in Spanish. I freaked out, ran into [a Catholic church], and Father got right on the phone. He's sent three of us here, and the other two are making it okay now.

Maria immediately entered the storytelling in that theme.

> I washed floors and windows to keep my kids with me, but a social worker squawked when I wasn't at home with them. If I'd quit the jobs, I'd have no money. That woman followed me like I was a criminal. She was just waiting for me to do one more thing she didn't like so's she could ruin everything I was working for. She kept saying I was a bad mother. I guess she wanted me to go back to the kids' father. He's a drug dealer. He tried to get me hooked. That's better for the kids? I went to the police, but they wouldn't arrest him; they said they needed proof. You know who told me about this place? A bum living in the park—on the bench next to mine. Since I've been here my advocate has done more for me than I'd ever hoped for.

Deni looked up from her coffee and grinned sheepishly.

> So I was wrong about the race stuff. The truth is, I had a good job, but my old man, he took all my money for booze—even after I moved in with a friend. He'd just show up and hit me until I gave in. [A longer story evolved about a particular incident.] I went on welfare and didn't tell him. Finally he figured I was broke; he couldn't find any money on me at all. I have to admit that all my welfare workers were Blacks and they didn't treat me nearly as good as the white gals here. That's the God's truth. Gerry, you add a bead for me.

As each woman assumed the role of narrator or auditor, she was continuously affected by how she perceived the others and her conceptualizations of how she was being perceived. Our stories as a communicative event included not only the unfolding plots, but non-verbal elements as well: gestures, tears, body movement, facial expressions, and social intent (Georges 1969: 313); Georges 1979: 104). The power of our personal narratives was not solely in its content; the act of communicating intimate details of our lives—while isolating images, or reaching out to touch another's hand, or shedding tears, expressing anger or fear—established a bond that transcended the mere characterization of experiences. Cognitively and affectively we were all involved. Each of us as narrator was stimulated by reminiscence and by the effects of our storytelling performance. Each auditor was engaged in a vicarious re-living of another's experience while being reminded of her own.

I had a specific purpose in creating the situation in which particular images and feelings emerged. I wanted the women to recall the crisis which led each to seek our shelter and the original and favorable perceptions of facility and staff. I wanted each of them to appreciate anew the necessity of our organization.

We had been telling stories for about two hours (during which time staff and volunteers passed the table) while Bob, the militant fourteen year old, had been circling, half-listening and drinking one soda after another—which everyone knew were only after-dinner treats. None of the mothers or organization members reproached him. He threw himself on the sofa and propped his shoes on the pillows. Maria, Bob's mother, frowned at his callous disregard for the furniture, and told him to remove his dirty shoes. He balked. Bob was not ready to relinquish his recent rise in status and power. He and his mother began a mercurial debate concerning his change in behavior. Her perspective had been affected by the storytelling session; he, on the other hand, only saw an advantage in his mother's rise in power and privilege which he did not want to dissipate. Maria reminded him of life at home with his abusive father, characterizing in story form incidents that brought back painful memories of situations far worse than their present living conditions. Bob became reflective; he did not put his shoes back on the sofa.

When I left that day, I wondered if there would be any lasting effects of the storytelling session. I returned the next day, bringing an auto club "trip tik" for Carol's impending journey. I was not warmly received in the office, so I ventured out to find the residents. Maria and Deni were conversing in the yard; they barely acknowledged my greeting. I found Carol in her room, unhappy. I dropped the trip-tik on her bed and left, passing Bob and four of the small children eating in front of the living room television set (which is not permitted). I concluded that my attempt to intervene had failed, and that now I was considered to be a traitor by the staff and other volunteers, and a fool by the mothers.

I did not return for two days. During my next shift I noticed that other volunteers were talking at length with the residents—in pairs, groups, or one-on-one. I overheard a new volunteer telling Carol a story of her recent orientation into the program, and how much the facility meant to her personally. Before I left, I asked two other volunteers what they had been discussing with the residents. Both had been telling of their personal experiences with the social welfare and criminal justice systems, and sharing common feelings and attitudes toward seemingly "uncaring" agencies. In all of the stories "our shelter" emerged as a positive force in the community.

The volunteers were telling more and more stories, the general theme of which was the facility-as-a-positive-thing. They were also increasingly becoming perceived by the residents as authority figures. A new power and privilege hierarchy was created.

1. The new volunteers
2. The veteran volunteers
3. The women residents
4. The children
5. The hourly-paid, part-time facility staff
6. The salaried, full-time facility staff

Within two days the mothers had resumed household duties with few complaints. Carol asked me to help her read the trip-tik. I saw the look of surprise on a staff member's face when she was invited to join the families for dinner. Relations were still strained, but more or less "normal" interaction and communicating were returning. Bob, realizing that his status had slipped, acknowledged the change and began to order the younger children to take baths, do homework, and "behave." When a recalcitrant child continued to misbehave, Bob took charge, telling a story of some incident which led to a "disaster."

Several days later I entered the facility to find the children at the table while watching television from across the room, the staff members reminding the mothers to take out the garbage and to vacuum, and the volunteers again in the buffer zone mediating during minor incidents. There was no blame-placing in regard to the crisis; instead, I heard only a few comments in reference to "the accident" itself. Once again, relationships between and among the mothers were somewhat strained; Deni, the black woman, took a discriminatory remark by Carol's child to be aimed at her, whether it was so intended or not. A younger child told Bob to "mind your own business." The power and privilege hierarchy had returned to its earlier state.

1. The salaried, full-time facility staff
2. The hourly-paid, part-time facility staff
3. The veteran volunteers
4. The new volunteers
5. The mothers
6. The children

The event lasted less than two weeks. I infer that the inter*group* dynamics superseded the inter*personal* relationships and individual perceptions within the social system. That is, what occurred in response to the crisis was generated more by relationships among groups or statuses than between or among people *qua* individuals. The residents, for instance, acted and reacted to the management groups (full-time and part-time staff members) as opposed to any particular person, and the staff members acted and reacted to the residents as a group, not to the individuals. I, and eventually the other volunteers, represented the only neutral stakeholders in the organization; we could be mediators—again as a group. My story telling(s) would not have been as effective if the other members of my group had not contributed their stories also. Storytelling may have been "cathartic." It certainly was effective in changing perceptions and attitudes, and hence behavior. Narrating seems to have been largely responsible for precipitating a resolution to the crisis, and for restoring a certain set of relationships making it possible for people to carry out their roles and for the organization to continue in a state of "relative equilibrium."

In "An intergroup Perspective on Individual Behavior," Ken K. Smith suggests that the "behavior [of individuals] can be viewed primarily as an enactment of the focus those intergroup processes generate"; in other words, "if an analysis is made at an intergroup level, a substantial proportion of the variation in individual behavior is explainable in terms of the intergroup dynamics" (1983: 359). Smith proposes that intergroup processes "(1) color our perceptions and play a critical role in determining how we construct our personal sense of reality, and (2) contribute to the emergence of behavior patterns that we traditionally label as leadership" (1983: 359).

In his description of the harrowing experiences of sixteen survivors of an airplane crash (in the Chilean Andes), Smith notes that the changing leadership behaviors which evolved during the ten-week ordeal must be understood as situationally-determined actions occasioned by altering intergroup dynamics. As conditions varied, new groups took charge, influencing the events and redistributing power. Smith questions whether leadership can always be constructed as a "conscious intent to lead," commenting that, in retrospect, particular behaviors which are deemed to be "leadership" may have been personal responses to the tensions of and reactions to changing intergroup interaction, consequently "triggering a new directionality" (1983: 359).

The situation in which the participants in the eastern organization found themselves was not determined by inter-personal relationships, but by intergroup changes. An intervention strategy had to be formulated to counteract the dys-functional restructuring of the power and privilege hierarchy. We—the clients and some of the volunteers—shared not only comparable problems and desired solutions, but also the realization that the facility was a community necessity. Storytelling provided the way out of a situation which the residents undoubtedly sensed as both a personal and social dilemma. The sharing of stories within the group of residents created a bond between them which had not been apparent before. The women found fellowship and hence the communitas which support groups manifest. The purposeful use of personal experience narratives is not restricted to intraorganizational interaction. This expressive form has an important role in interorganizational networking; storytelling between members of organizations who choose to or must communicate with each other represents mutuality of needs, aspirations, and commitment as well as a method to alter individual behavior and effect change in organizational direction. Such consequences of inter-organiza-tional networking will be discussed in the next chapter.

Storytelling as Interorganizational Communicating: Paradigms and Problems

(Recorded at a victims' rights conference in 1987):

"I've met *her*, but who is that?"

"I don't know, but all through lunch she was talking practically nose to nose with Doris Tate. Since Doris hasn't noticed us, and we certainly haven't been hiding, maybe we can become friendly with Miss Whoever and get into the inner circle through her. If we don't get some allies soon, we're going to be left out in the cold."

"I'm going to find the dinner steward and give him some kind of a sob story to save seats for us at their table tonight. We can bring up our little problem with [ ]. Our experience fits in with why *everyone* dislikes her, and we'll get Doris and Whoever on intimate talking terms."

"Listen, before you do that, just casually stop by [ ]'s table and get a conversation going about our desire to be in a coalition without [ ]. I'm going to get some of those terrific pastries and sit by [ ]. Maybe I'd better get a carton of them; she'll swallow anything as long as she's swallowing deserts, and let's face it, our tale of woe needs about half an hour. Meet you back here."

"Wait! Take some of our brochures. Let them just sort of stick up out of your purse. Drop one if you have to. And don't forget to tell that story about you and the senator!"

(For ethical purposes I have deleted the names of any person or organization who might be adversely affected. Doris Tate was a highly respected advocate in the California victims' rights movement, having become active after her daughter, Sharon Tate, was murdered by Charles Manson family members. As I have consistently pointed out, it is those who have been affected by tragedy or victimization who tell their stories, become involved with support group, and often create and maintain organizations.)

The two women parted to communicate their concerns and hopes to others by utilizing storytelling as a strategic method to influence decision-making. While they intended for particular stories to emerge, it is reasonable to assume that other stories were evoked during the exchange. It was noted by these ladies that *personal* experience narratives would be especially dramatic and could be used in subtle or brazen manner. They were attempting to build bridges to new sources of information, assistance, and power by sharing experiences which would establish advantageous relationships—and thereby be part of a resource pool in which their propitious linkage would supply personal and organizational premiums. They were networking.

Networking is an uncomplicated concept and is basic to human behavior: one seeks benefits for self and/or others by discovering and communicating with those who can provide enlightenment and resources. This participatory and negotiating activity is and always has been natural to the ordinary person in everyday life (one can even visualize cave dwellers networking by grunts and gestures to locate, kill, haul, and distribute meat to family or group), and it is therefore of interest to scholars as expressive behavior. Networking, like organizing, is not uni-level or uniform. It is a textured process depicted in the embossments and imprints of interwoven behavior (stories, jokes, rituals, rites, ceremonies, and so on) which may result in an established set of meanings, or be a continuing exchange of significant details which never seem to be completed. While the networking on which I focus is face-to-face interaction, it cannot be ignored that the 1990s find us involved in computer communication which provides a pseudo-face-to-face exchange, and I expect that technological advances will eventually allow individuals to see, smell, and touch each other through some other means than being within close physical proximity. That special relationship which exists when sensory stimuli elicit a weaving of what one says with the human factor is the personalization to which I refer, and which is the basis for a networking which transcends mere transfer of information. The personal experience narrative comes as close to letting someone into the marrow of one's self as can be accomplished through verbal interaction.

Networking may be so informal as to be unnoticed; women network everyday as part of their daily routine of shopping, personal and family care (visits to doctors, dentists, beauty salons, or health clubs), sharing community news on sidewalks or porches, church and school-related events, volunteering, meetings, and socializing at work, play, or luncheons. (Men, of course, have similar informal networks.) Often what begins as a temporary relationship becomes an ongoing networking, as in a support group. Networking may also be formalized and even mandated by work or an outside agency.

Networking in its most basic form can be observed in idionarrating: self communicates with self to obtain information as to the nature of the story in progress. Benefits accrue only to one person. When stories are being told to others, the teller and listener(s) are networking; their relationships are negotiated constantly as the storytelling event progresses, and benefits accrue to both parties. In an intraorganizational setting, individuals often network with other individuals using narratives as a strategy to influence, and groups network with other groups, negotiating for the most advantageous position through storytelling. When the minimal unit of analysis is the "group" there is likely to be a misunderstanding as to "group" behavior. Folklorists have approached the concept of "group" in various ways: societal, cultural, ethnic, religious, and occupational. While it has often been intimated that "group" behavior is indicative of members' behavior, Beth Blumenreich and Bari Lynn Polonsky address the issue squarely in *Re-evaluating the Concept of Group: ICEN as an Alternative* (1974: 15):

> What is suggested by folklore studies is that folklore is individually determined and based, not "group"

determined and based. Moreover, the individual's folklore is determined by the nature of his interactions and experiences. This suggests that folklore can be most profitably studied in terms of interactional, communicative and experiential networks—ICEN's. ICEN is based on a behavioral model in which people are conceived to interact and communicate on a first-hand, face-to-face basis. ICEN's involve dynamic human relationships which constitute the bases of experience. . . and evolve from the behavior of those individuals participating in the networks.

Networks, then, are explored in terms of communication and interaction. The networking process may involve a dyadic relationship or be established as "complexes of relationships, or sets of relationships between and among people" (Blumenreich and Polonsky 1974: 16). The benefits of networking will accrue to the individual and to the group in intraorganizational settings as representing the individuals in that group.

In interorganizational settings, networking is the manner in and by which information and resources may be covertly obtained, sometimes spontaneously exchanged, or openly discussed in a negotiation process. Networking, in effect, is a feedback and response behavior which may be expressed in differing forms.

William M. Evans notes: "All formal organizations are embedded in an environment of other organizations as well as in a complex of norms, values, and collectivities of the society at large" (1966: 33), and communication between organizational members occurs more frequently as the need for personnel, services, funding, publicity and change encompasses community needs. Therefore, the participatory and negotiating behavior of networking for one purpose may go beyond the rather simple communicating between individuals (dyadic, or within one organization, or between organizational members) to a more complex, multi-dimensional "webwork" of many networkings within a community, throughout the country, or, increasingly, internationally. The concept remains the same, however; one seeks benefits for self and/or others. An intertwining of benefits occurs which may not be traceable to its source. While the relationships which are sought by individuals in one organization with individuals in another may be designed to enhance only the one, it is natural that the benefits should *appear* to be of reciprocal value; the negotiative factor will usually break down if one party realizes that it will be dysfunctionally effected. Often the purpose of networking is openly meant to upgrade the status of some organizations while destroying others. This occurs when two or more organizations have the same stake in an affair and need to join forces to oppose other organizations. Coalitions are most often the result of networking which forges new linkages to address emergent or entrenched social issues.

While networking among organizations has been examined mainly in the context of structure (the configuration of organizations in a system and hierarchal patterning, for instance), research concerning interorganizational relations has been moving in the direction of the *manner* in which individuals and organizations formulate networks and the reasons for such needs. The field which explores how relationships are created in interorganizational networking which focus on social problem solving has been termed transorganizational development. A better description, perhaps, is presented by Frederick Thayer (1973: 12):

> occasions when individuals from different organizations and suborganizations work together to solve an existing problem. . . . The effective functions are performed partly inside each separate organization and partly outside, for the cooperative venture is itself a new organization. The emphasis on the "trans" helps us see that things occur both through and beyond individual permanent organizations.

The most challenging hypotheses and research pertaining to the ways in which the processes of entering into, maintaining, and improving status within interorganizational networks have been presented by David Boje (1983) and Boje and Terence Wolfe (1984). The emphasis is on understanding the process of net-working itself, which includes how communicating through metaphors can create a new language to redirect identities and roles, using storytelling to reconstruct the history and dramatic impacts of the network to "support alternative futures capable of meeting community needs," and the utilization of myth-making to "enable the network to gain control or influence over issues and align themselves with alternative stakeholders" (Boje and Wolfe 1984: 32-33). As they point out, myth-making to gain control over a situation is exactly what *advocacy* groups use as a strategy: "mythological qualities of the American value system are used to motivate stakeholders, mobilize individual and collective action, and invigorate the pursuit of shared goals" (Boje and Wolfe 1984: 33). This tactic is an important one in relating the organization to community needs.

While Boje and Wolfe and others suggest that a "change agent" (a consultant, or outside interventionist) is necessary to address and alter the meaning system of organizations and their networking processes, Boje and Wolfe refer to the "revolutionary" strategy of "bringing about change from within by working with existing stakeholders" (1984: 34). I suggest that this can be more propitiously accomplished without a change agent, but rather as a conscious strategy by those organizational representatives who have the ability to gain attention on the basis of their own particular personality or "star" quality—by the telling of personal experience narratives which contain powerful messages about the past, current, and future organizational abilities. The status of any organization is often determined more by its membership than its goals (for there are many organizations which espouse similar goals), and one of the most important assets of an organization is a "celebrity." Her stories are always heard; in fact people may *ask* for stories or opinions before she has a chance to offer either. A celebrity in a victims' rights organization may be a person who becomes famous because of a violent act perpetrated on a loved one (e.g., Doris Tate), or a movie star who has been the victim of an attack (such as Theresa Saldana, who founded Victims for Victims).

Having a "star" as leader or member attracts membership, provides entree to functions which might otherwise be closed, promotes opportunities for publicity, and facilitates the acquisition of power through important liaisons and increased funding. Stars are privy to information which may be private and confidential, or which may become available to other organizational units at a later time. Stars may also, of course, control information which is out-going, telling particular individuals or organizational representatives certain vital news while withholding it from others. Often this news is recounted in the form of an "I" story, a correlation between "I" the truthful informant, and some "truth" that must be imparted. The personal experience story is a favored strategy for gaining the audience of one's choice in everyday life and that audience may be in the place in which one works. Organizations are places of work; they may be factories, or offices, or groups founded for the specific purpose of advocacy. Robert Byington, in discussing the workplace and occupational group, labels the "worker who is most highly regarded by fellow workers, and whose endorsement and cooperation can open many doors that would otherwise remained closed" a "facilitator" (1978: 194). Robert McCarl refers to smokejumpers (an organization with shared symbols, values, and philosophy) who "both receive and pass a tremendous amount of information in both ideational and material form" (1978: 49). In their flow of information, "the oral narrative continually revives and maintains the equivalency structure of the smokejumper group by expressing the fears, joys, and concerns of the actual fire jump in an encapsulated form" (1978: 57). McCarl points to the "star" of the organization, the older jumper who must make his stories believable, especially to the rookies who look to him for guidance. The personal experience narrative conjoins the truthful "I" and the specific truths about the job that need imparting. The "star" *also* would be the most probable jumper to span the organizational boundary by telling personal stories which emphasize the importance of jumpers to those *outside* of the group. He would be their networker for favorable evaluation—and to gain benefits for the organization.

By combining "star" and "personal experience" with "organization," organizational audiences can interface. Individuals who have the ability to communicatively bridge the gap between organizations—as networkers—are termed boundary spanners in management literature, and have been described as "individuals who are sought after for advice and, in turn, influence the decisions of the less active members of the social system" (Tushman 1977). Eric Trist says they learn the "art of walking through walls" (1979). Perhaps it would be more appropriate to state that they have learned the art of *"talking* through walls"; they are heard (and believed) when others are not. The boundary spanner, or star, has the qualities of a hero: personal charisma, public recognition which may be accentuated by some distinctive characteristic, idolatry, a reputation which may include elaboration, and the diminuition of any negative traits. Stories abound about these boundary spanners; Anna Tabor of San Francisco told this story during dinner at a conference in 1986:

> Did you hear what Jane accomplished? ["What?"] Only what no one else could have done! She actually went up to Sacramento in her broken-down VW and walked right into the Governor's office and told him that if [ ] was paroled, she was going to fast in front of the prison until she died just like her daughter died out there in the desert for days without any water. Well, since her so-called husband—did you know that he was really a bigamist?—obviously killed the girl—his step-daughter, you know—is a relative of someone in high office up there [in Sacramento], he was moved real quiet-like to another prison, and no one knows where he is or whether he was released or not. Jane was so infuriated that she sat down in the hallway and refused to move until someone told her what was happening. I saw her when she got back from Sacramento, and she told me how the parole board had a closed meeting, which it isn't supposed to do, and now there's going to be an investigation. She's been asked to speak at just about every conference around, and I hear that "60 Minutes" called her. She's on the move! But, you know, the story is sort of mixed up. Some of the facts really aren't right as I've heard it from her and others. I wonder how she'll tell it when she's standing in front of a room full of people? I know it won't be the same as when she speaks in front of our group!

Stories also abound *by* boundary spanners, and often being a "star" is correlated with innovation. One "star" requested that I call her Anonymous; she refers to a 1987 conference:

> I had the chance to do something that I know I should have done, and I didn't. I guess I'm ashamed of myself. Remember [a particular conference] when that guy

interrupted right in the beginning of the meeting with an outburst about his lover being murdered and no one caring because he was gay? I sat there and listened to him ruining the whole two-hour meeting and I didn't have the guts to shut him up. We even waited for him when he stomped out of the room to get an article he wanted to read to us. And then it really didn't say anything homophobic at all. He started a discussion that had stupid consequences, that will last for a long time, and a lot of people were forced to support him. We were all afraid that we would seem to be homophobic if we didn't let him finish and then make sure that he felt that we were all in back of him. Damn! I should have told him and everyone right there about what happened to me at a conference in Washington. I opened a can of worms by mentioning a subject and a lot of conversation took up too much time and then I never got to what I was sent there for. My friends back home were angry with me and the legislation never got the attention it should have. We lost a very important bill because I didn't stick to the topic we had on the menu. I should have just said that we supported his unhappiness with the system and that we needed to improve it by moving along with our meeting. I was just too chicken to say that just because someone says or does something he doesn't like, that person may not be homophobic. But half of the people there were gay. Everyone's so damned sensitive that they're not being sensible. If I had said that—and I did have the ability to do it and get away with it—I think I could have straightened out that mess!

Being a "star" is not lost upon that individual; a boundary spanner has "star(wo)manship," knowing her potential and usually using it to her own advantage. An interview in 1987 led to this woman revealing intimate thoughts and:

It isn't always terrific to know that people recognize me. They associate me with something that's pretty gruesome if you really think about it. What do *you* think of when you see me?[I waved the question away; I did not wish to answer it at the time.] Okay, but I'm not letting you off the hook! Anyway, I feel pleased that I can go just about anywhere in our little sphere and say what I please and everyone listens to me. Most of the time they also do as I

suggest, which makes me feel good. Last month I was
asked to give a talk at a women's group, and when the
question and answer part came up, someone asked me
why I didn't make a movie of my life. Obviously she
meant that if I wrote the script, a real moviemaker would
make the film. I've thought about it, and it would be
flattering. And all that money! But I probably wouldn't
have complete control over what came out, and I might
look bad instead of good, the way I do now. I don't want
to give up what I have. Instead of the joke about E.F.
Hutton making people stop in their tracks and listen, *I*
really can do that. It's a great feeling, and I'm better off
now than *before* I was a victim. Does that sound conceited?
Then I guess I am. I am a hero and I *like* the power.

Just as there are heroes, there are villains in interorganizational networking. It is not surprising that they are also
boundary spanners; they wield influence that can destroy
relationships between individuals or organizations. Gossip and
rumor are their weapons. Sheila Roman describes how that can
occur (in a 1985 interview):

We had a good working relationship, Wendy and I. Our
programs were running smoothly and we had no real
problems with personnel. We lost a few to her
organization, and she lost a few to us. There weren't any
hard feelings because we had good rapport and we
respected each other. Then Kathy came along and when
she found she couldn't make all the changes in our
organization, she went to Wendy's. Kathy began to spread
the rumor that someone was playing games with our
books [funding records]. I didn't know that then, but I saw
how everyone became estranged at meetings. There were
fights that had never happened before. Then one night at a
coalition meeting someone said that Wendy was pregnant
and that Jack was the father. That nearly sent Wendy
through the roof, because it wasn't only a lie, Jack was
married. His wife finally heard about it and they're
probably going to divorce. Wendy blamed me. I don't
know why exactly, but I know that Kathy engineered the
whole thing so she could come back and take over the
organization. She may just succeed, too, because I can't
disprove that our books haven't been tampered with. We

have been losing money, and I can't account for it. If she hadn't spread that rumor, I know that everything would be normal. Of course I can't prove Kathy is responsible, but people listen to her. Aside from the fact that she has family money and influence, she got lucky enough to be raped by a movie star. She's been playing on that for years as if she's a privileged character instead of a victim like everyone else. But she has such a strong personality that she overwhelms you and tries to do it with whole groups. She scares—no, scratch that—intimidates people. She'll win every time. She's frightening.

Organizational representatives meet informally if there are work or play ties. Conferences are becoming more popular to combat such social and geographical restrictions. The phenomenon of "conference" is not new, but it has been taking on new facets of rationale and activity. As societal problems arise and affect populations previously untouched or unaffiliated (AIDS is a glaring example), people are more willing to join organizations—and have become more vocal at that level, especially regarding community concerns and legislative reform. The concept of activism is no longer restricted to what may affect *some* people, but has been expanded to what may affect any one of us at any time. Activism in the 1990s is more of a positive concept than it has ever been. Martha Purvis comments (in a 1987 interview):

> If my grandmother could see what I am doing, she would be ashamed of my behavior. And yet she marched for women's voting rights. She always said that *despite* the unacceptable behavior she engaged in, it was worth being ostracized. I listened to hundreds of hours of her stories about being punished for her activities, whether it was by family or neighbors or the law. I don't think that any of us today feel that we are being ostracized for gathering like this to plan how to stop criminals from gaining all of the privileges while the victims get shafted not once but twice. we're all here to see just how far we can go to stop victimization, and I think the whole country is with us, not against us. Lots more would come if they could, and just look at the variety of people here. We don't have anything in common except suffering from a criminal and the criminal injustice system. I see nods and smiles of

agreement from people on the street [she took off a large
hat, which was studded with buttons and badges, to show
me the slogans] when they read how I feel. Some stop to
tell me how they were victimized. *No one* ostracizes me.

It has become customary for conferences of this type
(which revolve around societal issues) to become a mixture of
celebration, ceremonial, and rite. Some have a "history" (as in
the 10th Annual Conference of Whatever) and some are the first
of many. There are "circuits" of conferences which are attended
by the same nucleus of concerned individuals and organizational
representatives. In all there is an atmosphere of perpetuity as if
the event were ongoing and the people had met before and were
continuing a tradition. "There's nothing new about being a
victim, " says Naomi Trager of San Diego (in a 1987 interview).
"We all know what has happened before and what will happen
again, so we all feel that we know each other and our problems."
Therefore, as people increasingly attend conferences devoted to
a generalized issue (such as victimization as contrasted with a
specific crime), the *multiple* problems that are discussed do not
separate the attendees, but rather bring them together in an
atmosphere of communal experience. Informal networking
begins the minute one enters the premises, signs in, and collects
an identification tag. One's organizational name alone may
institute the exchange of personal stories. To facilitate both
informal and formal networking, it has become the custom for
one room to be set aside for displays of (personal and
organizational) cards, brochures, and other "advertising" which
each organization is encouraged to bring. The printed material,
of course, presents another opportunity for networking; "the
story" of each organization is offered for all to read and relate to
if applicable. I had a table for my own material at the "Victims'
Rights: Opportunities for Action" conference in 1987. I was, as
Byington stresses, able to document technique and behavior *in
situ* (1978). Byington notes that the definition of "occupational
folklife" is what one considers it to be. I contend that the
conference is an occupational setting which, while a temporary
one, exhibits the interrelationship between the place of one's
"business" (in this case business means a place for the trans-
action of selling items—often handmade, as in sexually definitive

dolls which are used with children in counseling and court-related activities—and the selling of one's organization) and the attendant expressive behaviors, one of which is the art of networking in its various forms of informal gossip, rumor, personal narratives, jokes, and xeroxlore. I can present an emic perspective of the conferences I attend.

Every organizational representative at this particular conference (sponsored by the National Victim Center, founded by the son and daughter of Sunny von Bulow) had a stake in its outcome. The conference was held for the express purpose of advancing victims' rights by encouraging communication between those who knew each other and those who did not, and to foster collaboration among the diverse groups so as to form a coalition of victims' rights organizations within California. Most of those present were the activists in their respective organizations, taking special care not only to *wear* name tags which revealed the relationship between person and organization, but deliberately add to the pre-conference prepared tags by drawing the organization's symbol (e.g., "blind justice") onto the name card and/or using bold calligraphy to specify founder, president, or director.

Attendees capitalized on the symbolism of their organizations (e.g., by the wearing of a red rose [the "weeping rose" is a symbol of the Justice for Homicide Victims organization]; or a specific piece of jewelry [a clenched fist as formed in sterling]; or T-shirts with the organizational emblem; or slogans, mottos, and messages prominently displayed on badges [attached to hats, collars, upper body clothing, and handbags]). These occasioned storytellings about the significance of the particular item to the wearer—which provided informal networking via socializing and allowed the listener to learn of the teller's personal involvement with victimization and her organization. There was also attention to symbolic behavior in the form of "touching" as "togetherness": backslapping, too-long handshakes, hugging, and toasting with intertwined arms. This conference was meant to be not only informative but an emotional experience which promoted integration as opposed to fragmentation. It was a rite of unification to utilize the jargon of victimization: "his PV" (meaning parole violation); "he was GOA" (meaning the offender was gone on arrival); and "she was the V/W, but a 1385" (meaning that the case had to be dismissed; the victim-witness probably did not appear for the arraignment). Cliques developed, became the source of public and private socializing, and the joking relationships continued into the (serious business of the) meeting rooms for all to observe. A man with a harmonica played for himself in an isolated corner of one of the lobbies and soon found himself surrounded with those who crept from the meeting to exchange personal commentary or search for a bathroom; by the end of the second day there was a song created especially for—and possibly by—the conference members. (I tried to discover who the lyricist was but did not succeed. There was a similarity to an off-color limerick and had reference to former California Supreme Court Justice Rose Bird—who is renowned for her outspoken opinion against the death penalty.) Even through the music, then, networking in the form of projecting one's philosophies in lyricism was accomplished and available for creating new personal and organizational linkages.

While there were back-to-back speeches or workshops, much of the actual meeting time was spent listening to conference leaders telling stories of their amusing experiences with advertising or paperwork blunders and organizational opportunities gone awry. Many of the participants had similar personal stories to share both during the meetings and during socializing. These were people gathering for the purpose of publicly gaining recognition for their organizations as autonomous entities and to network with those who could strengthen such organizational power so as to be the nucleus of the new coalition. The most persuasive tool of all—for all—was the recounting of any personal story which would engross a listener in the interests, needs, and goals of the individual who was representing herself as well as her organization.

At the end of the first day the origin of every organization was known to all; stories had been exchanged and brochures read. The strategy from that point on, then, was to tell *other* stories of a personal nature which would exhibit extreme commitment under hardship, dramatize the importance of the specific victimization, display need or an arrogant lack of need, parade triumphs, discredit people or organizations, settle arguments, kindle new friendships, and indicate leadership ability. In other words, these informal interactions were proceedings necessary to the more serious work of aligning allies to concentrate power for any purpose which might arise.

Organizing was a challenge. The "experience" narrative was utilized as a tool of persuasion, whether for the good of one organization or the detriment of some other. Each representative was vividly aware of the competition for scarce funding and status; therefore the personal narratives were used to influence decision-making even among those who were longtime collaborators. It was especially noticeable that those who were already in cooperative ventures utilized mealtimes as opportunities to tell stories which might change opinions—and often linkages of power. The conference leaders were also sensitive to the need for good food, its aesthetic arrangement, and attractive settings surrounding the laden tables which encouraged sociability during a lull in the proceedings. I will never forget the huge bowls of hot fudge encircled by fresh fruit for dipping—which coaxed strangers to share space and conversation. People who had not talked to each other during the more formal meals, workshops, or meetings found it easy to establish new relationships while licking fingers and explaining how diets were going to be affected by the feast which could not be ignored.

Interorganizational networking thus presents paradigms and problems to be considered. The individual who represents an organization may be interested in personal benefits or those which accrue to her group. Usually a personal need does not interfere with the mission of the organization, and a personal experience narrative may elevate the status of the organization by facts which are unusually noteworthy. This is exemplified by Betty Day, a member of Justice for Murder Victims (JMV), who came to the "Victims' Rights: Opportunities for Action" conference to pursue her own fight to keep her husband's murderer in prison. She told her story to as many people as she could in an attempt to foster interest in the case, and she requested that all sign a petition. Her story did not conflict with the interests of the group, and it reflected positively on the organization. Her networking was evaluated as efficacious by other organizational members. On the other hand, personal narratives may not be evaluated as the teller hopes. The founder of Victims of Child Abuse Laws (VOCAL) came from Illinois to attend the conference. She distributed documentation of her case and avidly told her story to everyone. She expected the support of the other organizations. However, her story was evaluated as a poor representation of what other organizational members thought about the child abuse laws, and her networking reflected poorly on VOCAL as an organization. Her unfavorably received story and consequent image as individual and organizational member was compounded by other unfavorably received stories by several members of VOCAL. To illustrate just how devastating the results of networking can be, there was a very unpleasant discussion and consequent "scene" in the main meeting room and VOCAL was asked to leave the conference (never to return to another victims' rights conference). The image of the individual who has told a personal story, then, may also affect the image of the organization. This image projection must be evaluated as positive if the organization is to prosper in any manner.

A problem which arose at another conference depicts a situation which is not unusual. A personal experience story was told to a large group, and because there was a shared perceptual paradigm among the rather circumscribed membership who were appreciative of her organization, the teller received extremely positive feedback. She told the story to the right people in the right place at the right time. Flushed with success at the response and assistance she received at the first conference, she told the same story at a second conference—one with a varied membership which really did not share an understanding of the rather odd circumstance of her organization's purpose. She did not receive the feedback she expected, and because of immediate rude remarks and almost total isolation after her story, she left in tears. She told her story to the wrong people in the wrong place at the wrong time. What was an effective tool of persuasion to "sell" herself and her organization in one setting was destructive in the other; she had not assessed the contextual situation before she began to narrate. While one can never be sure that one's story will be appreciated by an audience, personal experience narrating is a *strategy* in interorganizational networking and one should be prepared for the possibility of disfavor simply because of the nature of the vocal conference. The repercussions for were far-reaching, and the organization did actually "go underground" for quite a while just because of her personal experience narrating. If she had been a star or boundary spanner, she would have had the ability to "talk through walls" and a group of newly identified victims would have had assistance. Unfortunately she was not only not a boundary spanner, but she represented an organization which was on the fringe of acceptance. Any organization which is on the borderline of acceptance needs an effective communicator. Celebrities are often born in that role. Cesar Chavez and Martin Luther King, Jr., for example, became celebrities *after* they functioned as communicators, and their organizational connections and social causes benefited.

In conclusion, from my observations and from what I have heard in the personal narratives of other organizational representatives, I cannot ignore the importance of the organizational boundary spanner. If that person is a "star," the organization must utilize that person's experience story as its focal point. Many groups have already found a "star" as representative, and the most effective "stars" are those who tell personal experience narratives regarding their relationship with the organization.

The outside "change agents" who have become popularized by management consultants to evaluate an organization's position in the interorganizational network structure would do well to evaluate the process of networking which the organization and its "target" organizations (which it wishes to either join or delete) utilize. By assessing the stakeholders who are both stars and boundary spanners, and having *those individuals* pursue personal narrating, changes from within the organizational structure can be accomplished efficaciously.

The optimal benefits of networking for the purpose of community planning is addressed in the next chapter, which will tie together individual, organizational, and societal needs in relation to victims (especially women) who have been rendered homeless.

CHAPTER SEVEN

Narrating, Transorganizational Networking, and Societal Needs

Lucy Poulin, of Orland, Maine, reveals how Homeworkers Organized for More Employment (H.O.M.E.) was established (in an interview for distribution to all who might be interested in H.O.M.E.'s development, published in H.O.M.E.'s newspaper: *This Time*, Fall 1985: 7):

How did it all begin? Well, I remember answering the doorbell—this is while I was still a sister at the Hermitage—and a woman coming in and asking me if I could help her sell quilts. . . . Out of Mrs. [ ]'s question we arranged a meeting at the Public Safety Building in Bucksport. Quite a large group showed up. And that's how we began—selling crafts. . . . [We bought an old farm and] we used the farm house for everything: sales, offices, inventory; it was a success from the start. . . . So when H.O.M.E. began, it was one of the first attempts to help people earn their living in their home doing crafts that had been a part of family history. . . . Many things strike me in retrospect. One is that I was enormously unprepared for the way H.O.M.E. developed. I think we could call that development, using an abstract term, community development. What it was was a mixture of social development, education, and economic development. . . . We needed a store. . . . We needed a school. . . We needed a sheep cooperative. . . We found an elderly woman who was burning charcoal briquets in her kitchen cook stove to keep warm, so we needed to find a way to harvest, fit, and deliver free firewood. Another need families have is for shelter. Out of that need we began to build low cost, energy-efficient houses. . . We wanted these to include enough woodlot area for a family to get its firewood, and a

greenhouse so a family could get food. The idea was that
the family could own their own home, grow food, and
have access to fuel. There's some economic independence
in that. . . . We also have three places where we give
emergency shelter: to homeless families, to battered
women and children, to homeless individuals.

Poulin is the founder of H.O.M.E. She is also the "star" of
the organization. She is more than just admired for her dedicated
work and liked as a person; she is revered. It is not simply
among her fellow community members that her special qualities
are noted; she is a boundary spanner. Public and private
organizations which would ordinarily be impenetrable to
personal requests for tangible and intangible resources are
responsive to her. Poulin is they type of networker that reaps a
harvest of benefits for *her* organization without intimidating or
jeopardizing *other* organizations. She is non-threatening because
her strategy is to utilize those personal experience narratives
which reflect the landslide effect of unemployment,
homelessness, illness, aging, and family deterioration—which
can occur in any order and do not necessarily include all
factors—and affect so many lives that relating personally is
almost assured. This strategy is both emotional and inform-
ational: given certain circumstances subsequent behavior and
particular results will occur. The listener may be subjected to no
more than a subliminal request for donations disguised in the
form of a humorous or sad story. On the other hand, the
personal experience may be so outrageous that the listener
becomes actively involved in a discussion of "what can be done."

Poulin has successfully implemented transorgan-izational
networking: interorganizational communicating for benefits
associated with social activism. Originally, her utilization of
personalized stories was probably an unconscious technique; as
a nun she wanted others to share her interest in the status of
one's "personhood." Stories of her own background and
empathy for what the poverty-stricken (especially women)
experience/exhibit a rare understanding of the importance of
maintaining personhood. As she became aware of the positive
results of her storytellings, it must have become a conscious
strategy, for she now encourages other (H.O.M.E.)

organizational members to utilize this same expressive process and form of gaining attention and persuading. Recent ventures in which videotapes and brochures use the interview technique to garner stories of travail to success by H.O.M.E. members have broadened organizational and community network bases, thereby increasing volunteer labor and donations for housing and expanding the economic structure.

Abbe Pierre (his name as a priest in the French Resistance during World War II) describes H.O.M.E. and its mission (in the Winter 1988: 7 issue of *This Time*) as

> a community formed among people once desperate, often without hope, who have found hope helping one another. The economic philosophy of H.O.M.E. will not be taught in the economics department of [universities]. . . H.O.M.E.'s founder, Lucy Poulin, has been slowly implementing her economic philosophy over the past eighteen years: use natural resources and native skills to build a local economy. The co-op started with crafts, selling the products of cottage industry and teaching the necessary skills from raising sheep and carding wool to leather working. Last year more than $250,000.00 of crafts were sold. . . . What we all share is the certainly that what life requires from us, as in a family, is that the smallest, the weakest is served first. If that doesn't happen, then the family dies.

Leavitt and Saegert (1984: 36) noted that their

> respondents frequently described their [New York co-op apartment] buildings as being like a family. It was the rule rather than the exception for more able tenants to look in on and help frail elderly or ill tenants. . .[In regard to mutual aid] people described the behaviors and related them to personal friendship or the fact that most of the tenants were good people. These descriptions contrast with reactions to the use of social services. Some respondents refused to apply for any aid. . . No one could be completely ignored or remain anonymous. At the other end of the spectrum, those actively engaged in the running of the building were intensely involved in social interactions with the majority of the tenants.

I have heard H.O.M.E. described as "a family" for many years. My first contact with H.O.M.E. was in 1971—when the organization was but a group of mid-Maine women selling handmade crafts in an old farm house on a desolate miles-long stretch of land between more affluent areas. In 1973 I was again driving along Route 1 in Orland, Maine, and I stopped to see why there was a crowd. A fair was in progress: food, pony rides, games, a roving clown, crafts for sale, and an auction. H.O.M.E. had three buildings that I recall—typical farm-type structures— and I believe it was that year that I noticed a small church in the rear yard. In any case, I visited H.O.M.E. every summer from 1973 to 1979. Each year there were more buildings and evidence of continuing entrepreneurship. I listened to those who lived "on the premises" or nearby and volunteer workers "from away" (Mainers' term for almost everyone who has not been a permanent resident from birth) tell how their lives had been changed by the development which had brought new meaning to the words "fellowship" and "community." I think that H.O.M.E. is an example of what Victor Turner had in mind when he explicated the term communitas: that particular bonding which transcends friendship among those who are sharing the same experiences. People in the Orland area who had been poverty-stricken were making and selling marketable goods to meet local and tourist needs—and were *living* together in community, but not in a "commune." They had space (acres) for privacy (and in fact many members lived miles from the main complex) and while each worked in some way in and for the group, they were not isolated in any sense of the term from the rest of society. Some had jobs outside of H.O.M.E. territory, and many networked constantly within and outside of Hancock County by personalizing the situations of poverty, aging, abuse, and homelessness and the ways in which they were dealing with resultant problems.

The organization which was founded and developed to assist local women in the selling of their homemade quilts now has on-site retail craft and food shops; daycare center; learning center and college program; flea market; sawmill; shingle mill; auto repair shop; horse training; shelter building and other workshops; distribution centers for food, fuel, clothing, and farm animals; transportation program; medical and legal assistance; co-ops for food, clothing, animals, etc.; museum; newspaper; homes built by and/or for the residents; and shelters for the abused and homeless. Everyone partakes of the emotional and economic benefits; they all recognize that without H.O.M.E., almost all would be in dire circumstances. General manager Nancy Upton said, "I realize how lucky I am to be able to live freely, have a home and family, and not worry about being thrown into the street" (1986: 9).

Upton and others whose stories are featured in each issue of the quarterly newspaper reveal that the status of one's personhood is foremost in one's thoughts; self is dealing with personal problems as well as how those problems relate to societal concerns which affect the lives of others. Folklorists might be the first scholars to note that telling stories of personal experiences is most effective in face-to-face communicating; one "feels" the other's presence and responds. However, the personal narrative does not lose its potency when told to an audience watching a videotape, nor does it divest itself of influence when in written form. The newspaper provides another networking forum for the revelation of victimization and "self" dealing with the consequences. Indeed, it is often the "untold" story (one previously told only to self: idionarrated) which first appears in print and has the dramatic effect of a sharing which subliminally requests feedback from *others* with untold stories and promises an empathetic response. A member of H.O.M.E. reveals (in *This Time*, Fall 1987: 1, 16) how she dealt with traumatic events in the past and how she wishes to communicate in the future:

> What I want is to go into poetry. Songs. . . . When I got upset I found myself writing. Writing about things instead of telling people. [She had already explained that she *couldn't* tell anyone in town about her personal problems because of embarrassment and censure.] That's why a lot of the poems I have written I don't show anyone.

The newspaper provided this unique opportunity for Karen to create a personalized scenario in which strangers could tarry to vicariously experience her life drama, relate, and appropriately respond to the organization which represents a haven for others who have encountered trauma. She was engaging in a transorganizational activity; her experience transcends her organization's boundary to encompass victims in society. In her journalistic enterprise, she was (and is) a boundary spanner. In a similar sense, memoirs, poetry, lyrics, and even graffiti have always provided propitious contacts for the furtherance of man's personal, social, religious, economic, and political needs. While the organizational term "transorganizational systems" is not familiar to folklorists, its meaning is; folklorists have long studied the individual in relation to his environment—which includes any groups to which he might belong, the feelings and activities of the individuals in the group, how the people in the group interrelate with "outsiders," and how social activism is effectuated through communicating. Hymes says (1975: 346):

> Folklorists believe that capacity for aesthetic experience, for shaping of deeply felt values into meaningful, apposite form, is present in all communities, and will find some means of expression among all. . . But our work is rooted in recognition that beauty, form, and meaningful expression may arise wherever people have a chance, even half a chance, to share what they enjoy or must endure. We prize human life.

Because I had periodically considered joining H.O.M.E.'s challenging venture from 1975 to 1979, that organization came to mind again in the 1980s while I was at UCLA and completing research pertaining to the successful habitational and economic structure of the Shaker Society. I wrote to H.O.M.E. to relate my interests and requested an update on the community's accomplishments. I expected a response from the secretary who handles the mail. Because I *personalized* my inquiry by introducing problems and issues which correlated with hers, Poulin herself wrote back to ask if I would be interested in the possibility of moving to H.O.M.E. to manage their new shelter for battered women. Our communicating was in writing, but there is no doubt that we were responding to each other through personal stories and those stories encouraged personal and organizational action. We shared the same perceptual paradigm regarding what was being said and what was *unsaid*; Lucy understood that my interest was not just in the receipt of "newspaper" information, but in how our concerns were meshing, and her feedback reflected rapport and the opportunity for action.

People find their way to H.O.M.E. because someone has told them about the *opportunities* available. No one (before 1970) considered that people in the Orland area had any *opportunities* at all. That word has become a metaphor for H.O.M.E. because the members have told their life stories to so many individuals and organizations that H.O.M.E. represents an escape from abuse, poverty, and homelessness to harmony, economic self-reliance, and a "private" place (as opposed to a mission or commune) in which to dwell. Personal narrating is itself an "opportunity"; it provides self with expression, and personal narratives let others know of opportunities both tangible and intangible. Without this opportunity to exchange ideas and feelings, there would be no collaboration—and collaboration is necessary to effectuate social change.

The stories which the H.O.M.E. participants tell hold the clues to the situations and behaviors in which abuse, unemployment, and homelessness are created, maintained, and perpetuated—and the means by which such societal problems can be alleviated. The question remains: why, then, are organizations and communities which posit and exhibit significant societal change not known to the general public as exemplars for shifts in perception and actual emulation? The answer is basic to our culture: the media is so powerful that a few people can literally control the way an entire population perceives and behaves. While the *Los Angeles Times* paid a three-day tribute to media impact of stories (October 24-26, 1992), I can reduce their topic to a simple example. A major article appeared about my work with the hidden, functional, educated, middle-class homeless in that newspaper in December of 1990. The editor stripped the reporter's superb article of the important sidebars which contained the ins-and-outs of our human resource systems, and the story that surfaced was a poignant piece about two women who were surviving by innovative tactics. It was not focused, as planned, on the solutions to abuse, unemployment, and homelessness, and it did not even paint a positive picture of women working out their lives in anonymity. I was not besieged by the foundations I had hoped to interest in innovative solutions to multi-faceted societal problems; I was besieged by requests from movie/television producers for the rights to *Shadow Women: Homeless Women's Survival Stories* and from talk show hosts who wanted me to bring along "a group of hidden homeless women." I turned down every television show except "60 Minutes"—the highest rated because the public believes that their broadcast journalists are the most ethical. I talked several completely undetectable homeless women into giving up their anonymity and participating on the basis of a breakthrough—"for the greater good"—actually telling the country how to solve our worst nightmares: rising unemployment among the highly functional, urban crowding and unrest, and increased homelessness among those who never have even considered the possibility of being indigent. The producers of our segment visited us twice to discuss what would be topics and what would be shown. Lesley Stahl and crew spent days taping us, listening carefully to our plans for creating new self-sufficiency, ecologically-sensitive communities. Our nonprofit organization was not only to be noted, but with on-screen address for donations of unused buildings/land and abandoned towns in all states for the beginning of the end of this crisis (societal) condition. When the segment was aired, we were appalled. Everything was deleted, including any mention of W.O.A.H., except the exploitation of women using public facilities to wash, apply make-up, and eat-for-free. They even showed one woman's license plate—a giveaway as to her identity. Voice-overs substituted for what we said and produced lies. We would have been better off by showing up on "Geraldo," sandwiched between dwarf-tossing and men-who-were-women-who-became-women-again. At least we would have been heard. There were no donations of abandoned buildings or land, of course, but seventeen men did track me down through CBS. They gave me their vital statistics and offered to take "the beautiful one" off the streets and into their motel rooms. If she was "already taken," then who else was beautiful and available? "60 Minutes" could have been responsible for the end of unemployment and homelessness as we know it today. But ratings were all that the "60 Minutes" producers cared about—and the exploitation of women was once again the favored means of garnering an audience. Remember the early reference to "women being more depressed than men due to their experience of being female in our contemporary culture" (Hearings Before the U.S. Senate Judiciary Committee 1990: 143)? At first it may have sounded ridiculous. But consider how women are still being treated. *We* certainly were not respected; the producers listened to us, viewed us *in situ*, and deleted all material that was the basis of our contract for agreeing to be interviewed. "60 Minutes" never responded to the many letters written requesting that the organization and its purpose be acknowledged. I put an ad in the *Wall Street Journal*, outlining the breach of contract and remedy needed. While the media has a lot to answer for, where are the socially-conscious attorneys who could have threatened CBS with a lawsuit? Is it just that they do not read the *Wall Street Journal*? Or, are our legal scholars so disinterested in community affairs that to step outside the ivory tower is unimaginable? This event would have been an excellent project for law school students who intend to pursue public interest law. Accountability should be enforced by those who have the expertise and ability to maintain the law and our quality of life.

Humanities and social sciences scholars could be providing research material that usually remains on university library shelves: the Shaker and Amish experiences in organizational development and self-sufficiency, examples of unusual coalition-building to defeat societal problems that fall under the rubric of transorganizational theory, and innovative programs on alternatives for batterers that may linger only as research projects delineated in disciplinary journals.

The NIMBY (Not in My Back Yard) phenomenon reflects a lack of awareness and education that scholars in urban and rural planning could rectify—just by hosting community "town meetings" in which slide-shows of successful alternative housing-and-employment projects are exemplars of progressive and excellent resources/living and actually upgrade the neighborhood. In addition, those academics and others from social welfare and sociology departments could be working within the community to point to the disparity of what and where human services are: the majority are clumped in very poor areas (often Skid Rows) where millions are spent for shelters, clinics, food outlets, and coordinated services—where only the underclass and truly brave dare enter or dwell. Women who have been living and working in middle-class neighborhoods will not take the long trip to an unsafe area where they have absolutely no ability to survive. It is almost as if the bureaucracy refuses to admit that the mid-city, middle-class is sliding into poverty and it is among this population in these areas that organizational and community response is needed. Scholars are available in every city to persuade those elected and appointed to be accountable for addressing the real issues.

My focus as academic-cum-community activist was to present H.O.M.E. as a model which could be developed in every state. I long considered that model as an independent one; in other words, I contemplated the establishment of similar but unconnected communities everywhere in the country. It then occurred to me that this is not the optimal use of the model at all. What is needed is the concept that these communities are organizational units in a multi-organizational format; a joint venture in which networking among the aggregate occurs for the benefit of all units. The communities will necessarily be different because of climate, land form and use, local needs, on-site expertise, populations, etc. Exchanging personnel, information, and resources would provide assets to all of the communities; they would complement each other. Like the Shaker Society, each community would retain its uniqueness and self-sufficiency but gain the advantage of the *other* organizational members' expertise through constant networking on both informal and formal bases. What I am now conceptualizing is a transorganizational system dependent on dynamic interaction to achieve a collective goal (eradicating homelessness and unemployment) by collaboration. The most effective means of collaboration is by narrating: educating while entertaining, persuading, chastising, and so on. Individuals would be sharing a reality based in shared (narrated) past and present experiences with shared expectations and actions. They would be "a group" with what would be perceived as a "group" output, but could only be assessed in terms of individual input: each person's distinct experiences contributing to the network. I realized that the paradigm was congenial with ICEN: Blumenreich and Polonsky's "interactive communicative experiential networks" (1974).

Each community would be populated with individuals coming together from varying backgrounds to engage in synergistic behavior to solve a common problem. Each individual would bring with him or her the experiences which would be communicated to the others. They would be networking with each other and with other organizations as stakeholders in a nationwide venture to alleviate the lacks of affordable housing and suitable employment. The undertaking would be an "experiential network organized for housing and employment": ENOFHE. (A loose pronunciation also provides the essence of life: "enuf.") The operative word is "organized," for *singly* the organizations—the experiential networks within each community—would not be utilizing their membership to optimum usage nor receiving interactive communication from other, similar, experiential networks.

As I contemplated the quintessential communities offering release from abuse, unemployment, and homelessness, I recognized the trap into which many community planning researchers fall: I was starting from the wrong end of the spectrum. Shelter and self-sufficiency do not begin with creative and idealistic models for dream homes and communities. The sidewalks and alleys and malls of every large city are roamed by ever-increasing numbers of homeless people who need practical strategies for immediate quarters and assistance which provide viable alternatives to swinging-door missions and inadequate social and economic services. Therefore, I developed a multi-level plan to accommodate every homeless person. I will discuss each level, beginning with the most radical—that which will remove individuals from sleeping on sidewalks and other indignities to "self."

Level One is a car park program, the elements of which have been identified by my field informants: safe, private, continuous, and weatherproof shelter with a legal address. This last is critical if the person is to be eligible for public assistance.

In every district there are compounds where unused cars, vans, campers, and even mobile homes are stored. There are also abandoned vehicles stranded in all areas. Everywhere there are vacant lots and odd land parcels (many of them government or utility owned) away from residential sections on which no "immediate" construction is planned. This land can be cleared and attractively fenced within a short time with the cooperation of council members who vote necessary variances. Manpower would be mandated by courts which daily provide alternative sentencing (for those convicted of crimes) to community service. Of particular significance would be the assignment of slumlords whose victimization touches the lives of the pre-homeless. In addition, model prisoners in county jails could be released for work detail. Thus, previously useless vehicles, cleaned and painted can be placed aesthetically among hastily planted hedges and gardens for pleasure or growing food. A trailer can house a resident-manager—a successful survivor of similar circumstances with management skills to maintain a healthy physical and emotional environment. Another trailer can provide food distribution. Portable toilets and showers can be used until more permanent structures are built. The minimal costs can easily be shared by public and private funding sources, and are preferable to the monies needed for the building of more (and unwanted) shelters—which perpetuate a "swinging door" mode of living and foster human indignity and abuse. This innovative program is especially important for women; the dangers of street living are heightened for them, and (American) females have been socialized to need privacy more than men. (One only has to consider public bathrooms.)

   Level Two is a trailer park program for those who are ready for more independent and longer-term living conditions but who cannot locate affordable housing or do not want public housing units. (These might be women who have been "successfully" surviving in malls, abandoned buildings, or cars.) Small, separated trailer parks on lots similar to the car parks (hedges and gardens) would accommodate "compatible types:" single men, single women, women with children, and families. Parks can provide some on-site services (e.g., child care, job training— such as bookkeeping and computer techniques—and counseling), amenities such as shared dining for those who cannot or should not cook, and spontaneous and planned social activities. Legal and medical services needed by the parks' residents would be appropriately handled by members of the Bar and Medical Associations who have been admonished for prior malfeasance or nonfeasance. A community would be established which would provide the better aspects of trailer park living while not seeking to compete with their expensive counterparts. Self-reliance and self-sufficiency would be encouraged by volunteers and those residents who already have the skills in the areas of resume writing, job interviewing, cooking, sewing, budgeting, and so on. In addition, the skills at each park would be utilized to build small structures for the sale of cottage industry products (traditional crafts which are very marketable as well as any item recognized as needed, e.g., decorative fencing), a diner with "home cooking" (again, traditional recipes utilized for economics as well as enjoyment), and any other skills, such as auto repairs. Networking beyond the park will occur as individuals seek employment, counseling, schooling, and legal and social services—and outsiders seek the residents for skills depicted in cottage industries. In time, each trailer park should possess the means for self-sufficiency. As residents move on and new people come into the park, more skills will be added to the conglomerate. The basic structure will depend on what the residents decide during regular sessions which will include the election of officers to manage park duties, and it is natural that storytelling will emerge as the means by which each person will enumerate his or her particular qualities and experience for any position. Using interpersonal skills will further ready the individual for employment and choice of living conditions. Just as storytelling sessions will occur in each trailer park, residents of different parks will convene to exchange information and resources, making optimal use of residential expertise.

While the aim is to accommodate all homeless individuals, it is obvious that the seriously mentally ill and those addicted to injurious substances will be excluded from the trailer parks in which those who can function effectively alone will live. That does not mean that other trailer parks cannot be devoted to the tasks of rehabilitation; Alcoholics Anonymous and other organizations would undoubtedly be interested in sponsoring and managing programs similar to the aforementioned communities with special counselors monitoring activities. In addition, unwed mothers who are faced with a decision to abort or become homeless may find communitas and self-sufficiency (leading to the ability to keep unborn children) in trailer parks devoted specifically to their needs. The costs of such trailer parks can more easily be borne by public and private sectors than alternative housing options.

The parks would be devoted to raising the quality of life and not conceived of as "temporary" in the same sense as shelters/missions; as June said to me (in a 1986 interview), "No one ever thinks that I care that every place I go is someone else's. I live with the fear that the next word from anyone is 'go.'" In addition, there is little to no incentive for residents of rundown and poorly reconverted hotels or those obviously sub-standard public housing highrises to put any loving care into their dwelling places. Aside from the notorious reputation of such residential units to spiral downward in disrepair and attract criminal elements as well as criminal attacks, the issue of how we perceive our space and utilize it needs to be addressed. Sara Serene Faulds notes that "our homes provide us with a freedom for personalization of the special places which we nurture into being, and which, in turn, nurture us" (1981: 54). The most telling comments came from landlords of the buildings in which the poorest live, e.g., "They don't take care of the place; it isn't my fault." Unfortunately, it usually is the landlord's-slumlord's fault for not providing housing code living conditions. However, the point is well-taken; if one does not have any interest (for whatever reason) in nurturing the space in which one lives, it will not reflect care. Certainly Fauld's comment "our homes are often places where new facets of identity and new ideas and skills can ferment, develop and grow" (1981: 54) is relevant to the opportunities provided by the trailer park program. Leavitt and Saegert report the "connection between one's sense of identity and social connectedness and [people's] buildings" (1984:36). Michael Owen Jones notes the process of utilizing one's own labor (which would be essential in the trailer park) as "gaining a degree of control over oneself and one's possessions, attaining intellectual and sensory goals, actualizing self through personally symbolic forms and achieving at least to some extent a basis for interacting and communicating with others" (1977: 13). Truly, this particular program will afford individuals an opportunity to return to a more wholistically participatory world in which their egos are enhanced.

I stress communitas and economic development. These hold the potential sources of reintegration. Communitas provides the opportunity for storytelling, the catharsis of which is healing, and reasons for action. Finding and keeping a job, locating agreeable living quarters, joining clubs, or going back to work or school need an initial process of sharing fears and plans with others of similar circumstance. Leadership and a growing interest in outside affairs will evolve naturally. Economic development serves both practical and image building purposes. It may also provide a source for matching funds with local public or private sectors. Such initiative on the part of the park residents will instill favorable self-image, foster a positive attitude and is preparation for an independent future.

Level Three is a distinct community such as H.O.M.E. In a rural area, land is available and buildings are either present or can be erected with local labor and resident skills. The growing of large quantities of food is possible. Farm animals can be raised for food and profit. In an urban area one must have vision: a razed slum or stockyard; an abandoned warehouse complex; vacant convents, monasteries, and church buildings; convertible commercial buildings; a group of affordable homes which can be "connected" to form a unit beneficial to the residents; closed schools and utility buildings; a highrise which can be managed by the tenants without interference; etc. My own feeling concerning urban community-building is that the religious institutions are being wasted; there are fewer men and women being "called" to God's service as celibates, and more "reform" religious people looking for social work to perform. This is a perfect opportunity for those individuals who choose to devote their lives to "God's work" to find a niche and influence their church officials to more appropriately utilize their service and the tax-exempt land and buildings. Networking is needed between church membership (ordinary households) and officials to effectuate this change in attitude. There are many very religious movie stars who could put their talents to use as boundary spanners to persuade the more affluent religious bodies to sell land holdings or build communities upon them, and convert under-utilized buildings.

It may seem that the rural communities have benefits which will elude the urbanites. In fact, each has distinct advantages. The farm-type community offers a wide variety of food and animal products for private and extended markets, as well as the aesthetics usually associated with greenery, ponds, space, etc. The urban community, however, has better business and employment opportunities. Wherever the community exists, the residents must focus on what the natural environment provides and needs. It is also important to remember that there will be people from rural backgrounds in cities and vice versa, so innovative thought and action is bound to result. (Some urban areas are still zoned for chickens, ducks, and geese, and there is industry in the sale of the animals, their eggs and feathers, and often in inspected meat.) Fairs (and flea markets), cottage crafts, antiques dealers, restaurants, theaters, auto repairs, clothing production and sales, and construction skills are desirable in both urban and rural areas. Mail order companies are marketing nationally regardless of regional origin.

Once there are the beginnings of communities, there must be a flow of resident communication. We are fortunate to live in an age of telecommunications, and conferences can be set up without the need for people to travel across the country to share their expertise. If hands-on skills are necessary, the traveler can be housed at any of the network of communities along the way. Stories of successes (or failures) at his home base will be shared as he progresses to the area in which he is needed.

A community member may desire to change locations. One of the errors that the Departments of Public Social Services makes is to assume that homeless people want to return to the place they left. In Los Angeles, many social workers cannot understand why the Return to Residence Program is not garnering more indigent people to take advantage of the free bus ticket "home." Some agency workers realize that Los Angeles County provides more in General Relief than other states offer, but most do not consider that if one were so poor that he had to leave his home territory, he has no reason to return there. (One of the stipulations of the generous offer of a free ticket is that the indigent person must prove that he has financial support immediately upon return!) However, if, while in one community setting, the individual desires to settle in another part of the country (possibly from whence he came), he can communicate that to the available settlements. Naturally, the advantage will go to one with some skill that is needed, and gaining such knowledge is an incentive for people to learn a new trade or become an expert in one he already knows.

Since I am working backwards, the last problem to tackle is how one can "create" a community. There is not just one way. There will always be individuals such as Lucy Poulin with a vision that somehow moves from one dimension to another. There will always be people who are grantwriters and find the appropriate foundation or corporation or governmental agency to fund a project. Movie (or theater or television) stars may institute a community by heading a fundraiser and following through with sponsorship. Wealthy individuals can donate their estates (or part of same). Churches can "re-plan" their land and personnel. Enterprising individuals anywhere can buy adjoining properties and invite residents of their choice. Homesteading in the sense of what existed in the 1970s and 1980s reality has been radically altered since the federal government halted the H.U.D. urban homesteading program. While there are still some rural (usually desert or otherwise undesirable) properties that are sold by public agencies that could be utilized as one's "homestead," the notion that one can purchase a prime piece of land (with or without buildings) for little money should be abandoned. The concept remains, however, especially in the instances of "homesteading" on land trusts (where the land is owned by someone else or a community and, if rules are followed, one can build/own or lease in perpetuity). The most interesting homesteading opportunities that I know about are on two small islands off the coast of Maine. Many year-round families have left the traditional fishing and woodworking lifestyle, and land—some with houses—is being offered (actually advertised) at low cost to those who formally apply and fit the qualifications for community membership. In other words, one must be "voted upon" in order to take advantage of this mode of homesteading. There are also new forms of housing being established in the United States on the Danish and German model of cohousing: many home units connected with common areas and meeting rooms, usually surrounding a parklike setting. This is not an inexpensive alternative to home ownership; the buy-in price may be cheaper than a detached house (urban or rural), but it is not what one would call "affordable housing for the poor." It is, however, one way to apply for grant money on the basis of creating a community within low-income urban settings.

Since cities and counties spend the most to shelter and feed their poor, it seems obvious that they would have the most to gain by combining forces and planning a conference of key individuals and organizational representatives to discuss how best to found a community. In this instance, a neutral mediator would be in charge of identifying and inviting the attendees, arranging for the conference site, creating opportunities for those at the conference to share equally in the decision-making process, and assess the data regularly. This is transorganizational development: a strategy to bring about *planned* change in the collective performance of stakeholders interested in the accomplishment of some deed which is beyond the ability of a single organization. This type of collaborative action is also developed under the rubric of what is termed Negotiated Investment Strategy (by Harvard and M.I.T. Programs). "Linkage" development is stressed, as for instance in how new projects can be tied to the social needs of a community.

From the stories that the homeless tell, there is a definite pattern that calls attention to a particular type of project. All across the country there are "dying" towns and farms ready to fall to the auctioneer's gavel. There are homeless individuals on city streets who would like nothing better than to live in a community atmosphere—or on a farm. Why not arrange for the towns to be populated with those who *want* to build a community rather than move to a large city (for that is mainly the reason the small towns are dying; young people are moving to "where the action is")? Why not arrange for those city homeless who yearn for a rural life to become partners with the farmers who cannot maintain their property alone? The homeless have not been living in a vacuum; they have skills that can be utilized to create business enterprises—whether in a small town or on a farm. (I am deleting the hopelessly mentally ill and addicted from this plan; I am referring to those individuals who are capable of functioning and are simply "down on their luck" for the variety of reasons which are revealed in their stories: factory layoffs, plant closings, family abuse, etc.) Every small town can benefit from new residents with a desire to create homes and build businesses. There are thousands of (often forcibly) retired people who have the interest and ability to counsel new entrepreneurs. No one has offered them the opportunity to "build a town." There are retired farmers who do not want to live in a nursing home; they can give counsel while being cared for on a farm newly created by those who need their expertise. Disabled people will be able to contribute to their own and others' self-sufficiency by the mutual exchange of ideas and work.

Innovative thought has not been brought to bear on the connection between the homeless (and pre-homeless) and rural and small town depression. I believe that my suggestions will alleviate much of the despair of city officials who expect ever-rising numbers of homeless on their streets and at their expense.

We must discover the abused and homeless before they do become so incapable of rehabilitation that these programs are worthless. There are visible and invisible pre-homeless and homeless populations. They can be found doubled-up with relatives or friends, living out of vehicles, in missions, shelters for the battered, welfare lines, jails, at unemployment and social workers' offices, in malls and alleys, on campuses, and in the courtrooms. Wherever charges are filed against abusers (wife or children) there will be victims who have no place to go except back to their victimizers. Teams of professionals in each city (or rural county) can be trained to approach these various populations to discern the most propitious manner of reintegration into a psychologically, physically, and economically functional lifestyle. It will be from the personal experience narratives that professionals will be able to glean desires to move to a rural area, or try a city trailer park, or make use of free legal services mandated by courts for attorneys who are guilty of any manner of victimization. It would be to every team's advantage to include a folklorist.

Bibliography

Affilia 4, Summer 1989

Allen, Barbara. "Personal Experience Narratives: Use and Meaning in Interaction." *Folklore and Mythology Studies* 2 (Spring 1978): 5-7.

Ammerman, Robert and Hersen, Michel, eds. *Case Studies in Family Violence.* New York: Plenum Press, 1991.

Bagarozzi, Dr. Dennis. "Using Family Lore in Therapy." *The New York Times*: "Style," 11 November 1985.

Bard, Marjorie. "Of Memories, Memorabilia, and Personal Narratives: Life Events in Introspect and Retrospect." *Folklore and Mythology Studies* 10 (Fall 1986): 42-51.

———. *Shadow Women: Homeless Women's Survival Stories.* Kansas City, MO: Sheed & Ward, 1990.

Bauman, Richard. "The La Have Island General Store: Sociability and Verbal Art in a Nova Scotia Community." *Journal of American Folklore* 85 (1972): 330-343.

Berk, Richard A.; Fenstermaker, Sarah; and Newton, Phyllis J. "An Empirical Analysis of Police Responses to Incidents of Wife Battery." In *Coping With Family Violence: Research and Policy Perspectives.* Edited by Gerald Hotaling et. al., p.159. Newbury Park, CA: Sage Publications, 1988.

Blumenreich, Beth and Polonsky, Bari Lynn. "Re- evaluating the Concept of Group: ICEN as an Alternative," in *Conceptual Problems in Contemporary Folklore Study*, ed., Gerald Cashion. (Folklore Forum Bibliographic and Special Series, No. 12. Bloomington, 1974): 12-17.

Boatright, Mody. "The Family Saga as a Form of Folklore," in Mody Boatright, ed. *The Family Saga and Other Phases of American Folklore.* Urbana, Illinois: 1958.

153

Boje, David. "ICEN Retraining Model: A Networking Approach
    to the Problem of Securing High Tech Jobs for
    Unemployed Minority Autoworkers." Working Paper 83-
    8, Behavioral and Organizational Science Study Center,
    UCLA, 1983.
Boje, David, and Wolfe, Terence. "Transorganizational
    Development: Contributions to Theory and Practice."
    Working Paper 84-1, Behavioral and Organizational
    Science Study Center, UCLA, 1984.
Brandes, Stanley. "Family Misfortune Stories in American
    Folklore." Journal of the Folklore Institute 12 (1975): 5-17.
Browne, Angela. When Battered Women Kill. New York: The Free
    Press, 1987.
Bryant, Dave, KTLA news (Los Angeles): 25 February 1987.
Bureau of Justice Statistics, Washington D.C. "Criminal
    Victimization in the United States, 1990." February 1992.
Buzawa, Eve. "Explaining Variations in Police Response to
    Domestic Violence: A Case Study in Detroit and New
    England." In Coping With Family Violence: Research and
    Policy Perspectives. Edited by Gerald Hotaling, et. al., p.
    176. Newbury Park, CA: Sage Publications, 1988.
Byington, Robert., ed. "Working Americans: Contemporary
    Approaches to Occupational Folklife." Western Folklore 38
    (1978): 185-198.
Cameron, Norman. Personality Development and Psychopathology.
    Boston: Houghton Mifflin Co., 1963.
Cantwell, Sarah. South Carolina American General Gazette, 1776.
Chesler, Phyllis. "Gender Bias in Court Determined Custody."
    Michigan Coalition Against Domestic Violence Newsletter VI,
    no.2, (February 1989).
Chittum, Samme; Bauman, Mark; and Nyborg-Andersen, Irene.
    "No Way Out." Ladies' Home Journal. April 1990: 128.
Court Review 28, no. 4, Winter 1991.
Cuomo, Mario. "Position Paper on Child Welfare." Coalition of
    Battered Women Advocates. (1988): 2.
Daly, Martin and Wilson, Margo. Homicide. New York: Aldine de
    Gruyter, 1988.
Darrow, R. Morton. Family Service America Report. Darrow
    Associates, 1987.

Dobash, R. Emerson, and Russell. *Violence Against Wives*. New York: The Free Press, 1979.

Dowd, Michael.: How We Batter Abused Women." *Newsday* 1 February 1991.

Dunford, Huizinga, and Elliot. Omaha, Nebraska study findings of 1990 reported in "Constraints Against Family Violence: How Well Do They Work?" Paper presented by Richard Gelles at the American Society of Criminology annual meeting, November 1991.

Dwyer, Olga, and Tully, Eileen. *Housing for Battered Women*. New York State Office for the Prevention of Domestic Violence, 1989.

Eckman, Fern Maria. Report of a 1989 study by the National Clearinghouse on Domestic Violence in Rockville, Maryland. "Battered Women," *McCall's*. November 1987: 159.

Eskeröd, Albert. *Arets äring. Etnologiska studier i skordens och julens tro och sed*. Nordiska Museets Handlingar, 26. Stockholm, 1947.

Evan, William M. "The Organization Set: Toward a Theory of Interorganizational Relations," in James D. Thompson, ed. *Approaches to Organizational Design*. Pittsburgh: University of Pittsburgh Press, 1966.

Ewing, Charles. *Battered Women Who Kill: Psychological Self-Defense as Legal Justification*. Lexington, MA: Lexington Books, 1987.

Family Service of Philadelphia and The Legal Center of Women Against Abuse. "Report of the Task Force on Mandated Counseling for Domestic Violence Offenders." (July 1991): 7.

Faulds, Sara Selene. "The Spaces in Which We Live: The Role of Folkloristics in the Urban Design Process." *Folklore and Mythology Studies* 5 (1981): 48-59.

Fellmeth, Robert. "Bar Procedures Do Little to Punish Incompetent Lawyers." *Los Angeles Times*, 3 June 1987.

Feminist Jurisprudence. May 1992.

Feminist Perspectives on Wife Abuse. Edited by Kersti Yllo and Michele Bograd. Newbury Park, CA: Sage Publications, 1988.

Ford, Judge James T. "Battered Wife Granted Right to Sue for Police Failure to Restrain Husband." *Sacramento Bee*, 10 January 1985: B1.

Frieze, Irene Hanson. "Perceptions of Battering by Battered Women." Paper presented at the National Family Violence Research Conference, Durham, New Hampshire: July 1987: 5.

Gelles, Richard. "Constraints Against Family Violence: How Well Do They Work?" Paper presented at the American Society of Criminology annual meeting, November 1991.

————. *Family Violence*. Newbury Park, CA: Sage Publications, 1990.

Gelles, Richard and Cornell, Claire Pedrick. *Intimate Violence in Families*. Newbury Park, CA: Sage Publications, 1990.

Gennep, Arnold van. *The Rites of Passage*. London: Routledge and Kegan Paul, 1909.

Georges, Robert A. "Toward an Understanding of Storytelling Events." *Journal of American Folklore* 82 (1969): 313-328.

————. "Feedback and Response in Storytelling." *Western Folklore* 38: 2 (April 1979): 104-110.

Gillespie, Cynthia. *Justifiable Homicide: Battered Women, Self-Defense, and the Law*. Columbus, OH: Ohio State University Press, 1989.

Greene, Maury. "The Skid Row Sweeps: Staking Out Positions." *Los Angeles Times*, 25 February 1987.

Grossman, Jody. *Domestic Violence and Incarcerated Women: Survey Results*. New York State Department of Correctional Services. October (1985): 8.

Hand, Wayland D., founder. *Encyclopedia of American Popular Beliefs and Superstitions*. Edited by Donald Ward. University of California Press, forthcoming.

Handbook of Family Violence. Edited by von Haselt et. al. New York: Plenum Press, 1988.

Hansen, Marsali; Harway, Michele; and Cervantes, Nancyann. "Therapists' Perceptions of Severity in Cases of Family Violence." *Violence and Victims* 6, no.3, 1991.

Harlow, Caroline. "Female Victims of Violent Crimes." Bureau of Justice Statistics, Washington, D.C. : U.S. Department of Justice (1991): 6.

Hemminger, Helen. *A Study of the Former Guests of a Homeless Shelter*. Executive Summary, Wellspring House Inc. Gloucester, MA, 1991.

Hirschel, David; Hutchison, Ira; and Dean, Charles. "The Failure of Arrest to Deter Spouse Abuse." *Journal of Research in Crime and Delinquency* 29, no. 1, February 1992.

Honko, Lauri. *Geisterglaube in Ingermanland*. FF Communications, 185 (Helsinki, 1962).

———. "Empty Texts, Full Meanings on Transformal Meaning in Folklore," in Kvideland, Reimund, ed. *Papers I-IV; Plinary Papers: the 8th Congress for the International Society for Folk Narrative Research*, Bergen, 1984: 273-281.

Hufford, David. *The Terror That Comes in the Night: An Experience-Centered Study of Assault Traditions*. Philadelphia: University of Pennsylvania Press, 1982.

Huling, Tracy. "Breaking the Silence." *The Correctional Association of New York*. (March 1991).

Humphrey, Linda. "Small Group Festive Gatherings." *Journal of the Folklore Institute* 16 (1979): 190-201.

Hymes, Dell. "Folklore's Nature and the Sun's Myth." *Journal of American Folklore* 88 (1975): 345-369.

International Journal of Health and Services 20, no.1, 1990.

Ives, Edward. *Joe Scott: The Woodsman Songmaker*. Urbana: University of Illinois Press, 1978.

Jaffe, Peter; Wolfe, David A.; and Wilson, Susan Kaye. *Children of Battered Women*. Newbury Park, CA: Sage Publications, 1990.

Jones, Ann. *Women Who Kill*. New York: The Fawcett Crest, 1980.

Jones, Michael Owen. *The Handmade Object and Its Maker*. Los Angeles: University of California Press, 1975.

———. "L.A. Add-ons and Re-dos: Private Space vs. Public Policy." Paper presented at Popular Culture Association/West Conference, UCLA, 1977.

Jones, Michael Owen; Moore, Michael Dane; and Snyder, Richard Christopher, eds. *Inside Organizations: Understanding the Human Dimension*. Newbury Park, CA Sage Publications, 1988.

Jonsen, Dr. Albert. "Altering Nature: Ethics in the Bio-Revolution." *Humanities Network*, Vol. 9: 1 (1987).

Journal of Family Violence 6, no.1, 1991.

Kalcik, Susan. "'. . .like Ann's gynecologist or the time I was almost raped': Personal Narratives in Women's Rap Groups." *Journal of American Folklore* 88 (1975): 3-11.

Kuhl, Anna and Saltzman, Linda E. "Battered Women and the Criminal Justice System." In The Changing Roles of Women in the Criminal Justice System: Offenders, Victims, and Professionals. Edited by Imogene L. Moyer. Prospect Heights, IL: Waveland Press Inc. , 1985.

Kurz, D. and Coughey, K. "The Effects of Marital Violence on the Divorce Process." Paper presented at the American Sociological Association meeting, August 1989.

Law and Society Review 23, no.1, 1989.

Leavitt, Jacqueline and Saegert, Susan. "Women and Abandoned Buildings." *Social Policy* 15 (1984): 32- 38.

Levy, Barrie. *Skills for Violence-Free Relationships.* Los Angeles: Southern California Coalition on Battered Women, 1985.

Los Angeles Times. "Permanent Homes Give Battered Women Time to Change Their Lives." 18 November 1990: Q 37

———. "Living in the Shadows." 2 and 30 December 1990: E1.

———."Abused Women May Be Hostages." 20 August 1991: E1.

———. "Media Impact: Why Does a Story Grab Public's Notice?" 24-26 October 1992.

———. "Program Aims at Violence on Women." 24 May 1993: B2.

Mahoney. "Legal Images of Battered Women." *Michigan Law Review* 1, 1991: 39.

Maryland: "Adoption of New Rules for Lawyers Recommended," *The Jeffersonian,*11 May 1985.

Maryland Court of Appeals. *Study of the American Bar Association Model Rules of Professional Conduct:* 1983.

Maryland Family Violence Coalition. "Broken Bodies and Broken Spirits: Family Violence in Maryland and Recommendations for Change." June 1991.

McCarl, Robert. "Smokejumper Initiation: Ritualized Communication in a Modern Occupation." *Journal of American Folklore* 89 (1976): 46-67.

Mederer, Helen J. and Gelles, Richard J. "Compassion or Control: Intervention in Cases of Wife Abuse." *Journal of Interpersonal Violence* 4, no. 1, March (1989): 25.

Mediation Quarterly 9, no.3, Spring 1992.

Merrill, Cindy. "Death Ends Ordeal For One Woman." *The Houston Post* 16 October 1989: A10.

Mitroff, Ian. *Stakeholders of the Organizational Mind.* San Francisco: Jossey-Bass, 1983.

Morgan, Kay. "Reassessing the Battery of Women: A Social and Economic Perspective." *Feminist Jurisprudence.* May 1992.

Myerhoff, Barbara. "Telling One's Story." *The Center Magazine* 13 (1980): 22-43.

———. *Number Our Days.* New York: Simon and Schuster, 1978.

NCADV Voice. Newsletter of the National Coalition Against Domestic Violence. 1989.

National Criminal Justice Association (NCJA) Justice Research. "States, Federal Government Increasing Focus on Violence Against Women." September/October (1990): 3.

Neidig, Peter. "Women's Shelters, Men's Collectives and Other Issues in the Field of Spouse Abuse." *Victimology* 9 (1984): 464-474.

New York Times. Schmitt, "Family Violence: Protection Improves But Not Prevention." 17 January 1989: B1.

Nilsson, Albert. *"Intressedominanz und Volksüberlieferung, Einige Uberlieferungspsychologische Gesichtspunkte."* *Acta Ethnologica, Kobenhavn,* 1936: 165-186.

Otto, Rudolf. *Das Heilige: Uber das Irrationale in der Idee des Gottlichen,* 30th ed. (Munchen, 1936).

Pence, Ellen et al. "Response to Peter Niedig's Article: 'Women's Shelters, Men's Collectives and Other Issues in the Field of Spouse Abuse." *Victimology* 9 (1984): 477-482.

Pettigrew, Andrew. "On Studying Organizational Cultures." *Administrative Science Quarterly* 24 (1979):570-581.

Philadelphia Inquirer. Report by the Legal Center of Women Against Abuse: "North Philadelphia Taking Aim at Domestic Violence." 21 July 1992: B1.

Pierre, Abbe. *This Time.* Winter 1988.

Planned Parenthood of Southeastern Pennsylvania v. Robert Casey. Supreme Court of the United States, 1992: 34, no. 290-291.

Poulin, Lucy. *This Time*. Fall 1985.

Report to the Task Force for Legal Services to the Needy, Pennsylvania Bar Association. December 1990: 25.

Response 12, no. 4, 1989.

The River. "Grim Tally." Texas, January/February 1992.

Santino, Jack. "Characteristics of Occupational Narrative." *Western Folklore* 37: 199-212.

Scott, Eugene. Father's Day Message, 1987 (and other videotaped programs from channels 30 and 56 in Los Angeles).

Siegal, Mark; Nancy Jacobs, and Carol Foster, eds. *Domestic Violence: No Longer Behind the Curtains*. Wylie, Texas, 1989.

Simpson, Jacqueline. *The Folklore of Sussex*. London: B.T. Batsford Ltd., 1973.

Smith, Ken. "an Intergroup Perspective on Individual Behavior," in Hackman, Lawler and Porter, eds. *Perspectives on Behavior in Organizations*. New York: McGraw-Hill, 1983: 359-372.

Social Problems. Vol. 39, No.1, February 1992.

Sonkin, Daniel, ed. *Domestic Violence on Trial: Psychological and Legal Dimensions of Family Violence*. New York: Springer Publishing Company, 1987.

Sonkin, Daniel; Martin, Del; and Walker, Lenore. *The Male Batterer: A Treatment Approach*. New York: Springer Publishing Company, 1985.

Stahl, Sandra K.D. "The Personal Narrative as Folklore." *Journal of the Folklore Institute* 14 (1977): 9-30.

————."Personal Experience Stories." In *Handbook of American Folklore*. Edited by Richard Dorson. Bloomington: Indiana University Press, 1983.

————."Interpreting Personal Narrative Texts." In *Literary Folkloristics and the Personal Narrative*. Bloomington: Indiana University Press, 1989.

Stark, Evan and Flitcraft, Anne. "Violence Among Intimates: An Epidemiological Review." In *Handbook of Family Violence*. Edited by von Haselt et. al., p. 303. New York: Plenum Press, 1988.

Stern, Gerald M. "From Chaos to Responsibility." *American Journal of Psychiatry* 133 March 1976: 300-301.

Stewart, Susan. "The Epistemology of the Horror Story." *Journal of American Folklore* 95 (1981): 33-50.

Straus, Murray and Gelles, Richard. *Physical Violence in American Families: Risk Factors and Adaptations to Violence in 8,145 Families.* 1990: 426.

Surgeon General's Workshop on Violence and Public Health Source Book. Leesburg, Virginia. October 1985.

Sydow, Carl von. *Die psychologischen Gründe der Mana-Vorstellung. Vetenskapssocietetens i Lund arsbok, Lund,* 1929.

———. *Selected Papers on Folklore.* Copenhagen, 1948.

Taub, Nadine. "Adult Domestic Violence: The Law's Response." *Victimology* 8 (1983): 152-171.

Thayer, Frederick G. *An End to Hierarchy! An End to Competition!* New York: Franklin Watts, 1973.

Thompson, Stith. *Motif-Index of Folk-Literature.* 2nd ed. 6 vols. 1955-1958.

———. *The Folktale.* Berkeley: University of California Press, 1946.

Thyfault, Roberta K. "Self-Defense: Battered Woman Syndrome on Trial," *California Western Law Review* 20 (1984): 490.

Trist, Eric. "Referent Organizations and the Development of Interorganizational Domains." Distinguished Lecture to the Academy of Management 39th Annual Convention, Atlanta, (1979).

Turner, Victor. *The Ritual Process: Structure and Anti-structure.* Chicago: Aldine, 1969.

———. *Dramas, Fields, and Metaphors.* Ithaca: Cornell University Press, 1974.

Tushman, Michael. "Special Boundary Roles in the Innovation Process." *Administrative Science Quarterly* 22 (1977): 587-603.

U.S. Conference of Mayors: news release. 29 April 1986.

U.S., Congress, Senate, "Women and Violence." *Hearings Before the U.S. Senate Judiciary Committee,* August 29 and December 11, 1990, Senate Hearing 101-939, Parts 1 and 2.

U.S., FBI. *Los Angeles Times. 26 July 1987.*

Van de Kamp, John. "Bar Procedures Do Little to Punish Incompetent Lawyers." *Los Angeles Times*. 3 June 1987.

Viano, Emilio. "Victimology: The Development of a New Perspective." *Victimology* 8 (1983): 17-30.

———."Victimology: The Study of the Victim." *Victimology* 1 (1976): 1-7.

Vilmur, Robert G. "U.S. Conference of Mayors Cites Los Angeles as Homeless Numbers Rise." *Los Angeles Times*. 17 December 1986.

Violence and Victims 5, no.4, 1990.

Violence Update 1, no.6, February 1991.

Wachs, Eleanor. "The Crime-Victim Narrative as a Folkloric Genre." *Journal of the Folklore Institute* 19 (1981): 17-30.

Walker, Lenore. *The Battered Woman*. New York: Harper & Row, 1979.

———. *The Battered Woman Syndrome*. New York: Springer Publishing Company, 1984.

———. *Terrifying Love: Why Battered Women Kill and How Society Responds*. New York: Harper & Row, 1989.

Ward, Donald. "The Little Man Who Wasn't There: On the Perception of the Supranormal." *Fabula* 18 (1977): 212-225.

———. "The Performance and Perception of Folklore and Literature." *Fabula* 20 (1979): 256-264.

———. "The Return of the Dead Lover: Psychic Unity and Polygenesis Revisited." *Folklore on Two Continents*, Burlakoff, ed. Bloomington: Trickster Press, 1980: 310-317.

Wilson, Lydia. *South Carolina Gazette*: 28 October 1764.

Women's Rights Law Reporter 9, 1986.

Zorza, Joan. "The Gender Bias Committee's Domestic Violence Study: Important Recommendations and First Steps." 33 *Boston Bar* J.4, 13, July/August 1989.

Index

activism 92, 95, 125, 134, 138
American Association for
  Marriage and Family
  Therapy 65
American Psychological
  Association 46
Andersen, Dotty 87
archetype 57
Attorney Grievance Commission
  16, 77, 106

"battered woman syndrome " 5
Bauman, Richard 89, 91, 93, 95
blame-placing 101, 111
Blumenreich, Beth 117, 118, 143
Boatright, Mody 60
Boje, David 119, 120
boundary spanner 121, 122, 123,
  124, 131, 134, 138, 148
Brandes, Stanley 60
brief reactive psychosis 5
Bryant, Dave 20
Buffalo Creek 21
Byington, Robert 121, 126

Cantwell, Sarah 4, 6
catharsis 25
Children of Murdered Parents 90
Coalition of Organizations and
  People (CO-OP) 90
communitas 19, 20, 21, 22, 39, 65,
  66, 89, 113, 136, 146, 147
community 3, 7, 15, 17, 20, 21, 24,
  87, 91, 94
conferences 93
coping mechanism 19
corruption 17
couples-therapy 10
criminology 12

Cuomo, Mario 7

Davis, Coleen 90
Defiant Victims of Incest 88
depression 6, 25, 53, 151
diagnosis 6
Dobash, Drs. R. Emerson and
  Russell 8
domestic abuse 6, 7, 8, 17, 18, 19,
  39, 56, 58, 61, 72, 75, 76, 84
The Domestic Violence Legal
  Clinic 76
Donovan, Mary Alice 41, 42

economic development 133, 147
Evans, Sally 85, 86

family misfortune stories 60
family myths 65
Family Service America 11
family therapists 65
Family Violence Coalition 76, 77
feedback and response 35, 45, 97,
  118
fellowship 21,22, 27, 90, 92, 113,
  136
folklorist 27, 47, 61, 65, 78, 117,
  137, 138
folktales 63
Frieze, Irene Hanson 37

Gelles, Richard 52, 53, 73, 74
Georges, Robert A. 34, 35, 36, 109
Gestalterganzung 54

"hag" 47
"hagging" 48, 50, 51, 52, 53, 56
Hearings before the U.S. Senate
  74, 141

hidden homeless women 140
hierarchy of power and privilege
    99
Holocaust 36
homesteading 149, 150
Homeworkers Organized for
    More Employment
    (H.O.M.E.) 133, 134, 135, 136,
    137, 138, 139, 141, 142, 147
Honko, Lauri 54, 78
House of Ruth 77
Hufford, David 48, 49
Hymes, Dell 43, 138
hypnagogic 53, 57

ICEN 117, 118, 143
Idionarrating 27, 28, 30, 34, 35
indemnification 26
interorganizational networking
    119, 129, 131
intervention 97
intraorganizational crisis 97
isolation 6, 13, 21, 30, 38, 45, 87,
    92, 130

Jones, Ann 5
Justice for Homicide Victims
    127(JHV)
Justice for Murder Victims (JMV)
    129
Justiceville 23

Kalcik, Susan 94

La Have Island general store 89,
    91, 93
Leavitt, Jacqueline 24, 135, 146
Legal Aid 107
liminality 22, 23
Los Angeles Times 9, 46, 74, 139
Love Camp 20, 21

malfeasance 15, 16, 76
McGuire, Mary 5
methodology 9
Minnesota Domestic Abuse
    Intervention Project 10
Mitroff, Ian 57
Mothers Against Drunk Drivers
    (MADD) 95
Motif-Index of Folk-Literature 62
murder 7, 9, 37, 90, 116, 123

Myerhoff, Barbara 27, 30, 31, 36

Narrators:
    Adriana 50, 51
    Amy 51, 54
    Ann 71
    Annie 67, 68, 69
    Bettina 60
    Bryant, Dave 20
    Carlotta 67
    Carol 100, 101, 105, 106, 107, 110
    Carolyn 67
    Dave 20
    Deni 100, 105, 107, 108, 110
    Donna 14
    Eddie 20
    Eve 55
    Fragan, Mr. 61, 63
    Fragan, Mrs. 61
    Geraldine 100, 101, 105, 106, 107
    Harry 22
    Janie 42
    Jennie 37
    Mac the Hermit 64, 65
    Margaret 70
    Maria 53, 100, 101, 104, 105, 108,
        109, 110
    Marie 58
    Patty 29
    Pauley, Mr. 62
    Pauley, Mrs. 62
    Poulin, Lucy 133, 134, 135, 138,
        149
    Rachel 59, 69
    Reggie 32, 33
    Ricky 44, 45
    Sandi 31, 43
    Teddy 22

National Clearinghouse on
    Domestic Violence 76, 77
National Organization for
    Women (N.O.W.) 76, 106
National Victim Center 127
National Woman Abuse
    Prevention Project 76
Negotiated Investment Strategy
    150
Neidig, Peter 10
networking 90, 113, 116, 117, 118,
    124, 126, 127, 138, 129, 131,
    137, 142, 143, 147

NIMBY (Not in My Back Yard) 141

"Old Hag" 47, 48, 49
"overnight indigency" 7

Parents of Murdered Children 90 (PMC)
Pence, Ellen 10, 15
Pierre, Abbe 135
personal experience narratives 26, 39, 43, 73, 87, 92, 97, 113, 116, 131, 134, 151
personal space 100
personhood 5, 25, 26, 28, 34, 134, 137,
Planned Parenthood 6
police 6, 16, 20, 73, 74, 75, 104, 105
Polonsky, Bari Lynn 117, 118, 143
post-traumatic stress disorder 5
Poulin, Lucy 134, 138
power and privilege hierarchy 102, 110, 111

recidivism 7, 69, 72, 73
retaliation 6, 14
"Rule of Thumb" 4
rural communities 148

Saegert, Susan 24, 135, 146
Saldana, Theresa 120
self-esteem 13, 35, 103
sexual connotation 49, 56
Shaker Society 138, 142
shared perceptual paradigm 94, 130
shelter 9, 23, 99, 103, 142, 143, 151
"60 Minutes" 140, 141
skid rows 14, 142
Smith, Ken K. 112
South Carolina American General Gazette 4
South Carolina Gazette 3
Southern California Coalition on Battered Women 17
Special Joint Committee on Gender Bias in the Courts 76
stakeholders 20, 57, 111, 120, 131, 143, 150
"star" 120, 121, 122, 123, 134
Stewart, Susan 83

storytelling 25, 28, 34, 36, 66, 83, 92, 111, 112, 116, 117, 145
suicide 7, 9, 71, 104
Sunny von Bulow National Victim Center 95
supranormal experience 12, 25, 47, 52

Tabor, Anna 122
Tate, Doris 115, 116, 120
Tate, Sharon 116
Taub, Nadine 11, 16
"Threshold people" 19
town meetings 69, 77, 141
Turner, Victor 18,19, 22, 136

Upton, Nancy 137
U.S. Centers for Disease Control and Prevention 11

van Gennep, Arnold 18
Verna 32
Viano, Emilio 3, 12, 13, 14, 15
victimology 3, 12, 17
Victims for Victims 122
Victims of Child Abuse Laws (VOCAL) 130
victims' support groups 91
von Bulow, Sunny 127
von Bulow, Klaus 127
von Sydow, Carl 38

Wachs 12, 13, 32
Walker, Lenore 9, 17, 73, 74
Wall Street Journal 141
Ward, Donald 56, 94, 95
Wolfe, Terence 119, 120
Women Against Abuse in Philadelphia 9
Women Against Abuse Legal Center 74
Women Organized Against Homelessness, (W.O.A.H.) 75, 140
Women's Rights Litigation Clinic 11